ALSO BY ROSALYN DREXLER

Starburn
The Cosmopolitan Girl
To Smithereens
One or Another
I Am the Beautiful Stranger

# BAD GUY

*This book is dedicated to the memory of my father, George Bronznick (Klemuns), who died November 6, 1980, at the age of seventy-seven, and was buried under a maple tree. I loved him.*

# BAD GUY

# 1

"Imagine a humid July afternoon."

"Human?"

"Humid!"

"So what about it?"

"Imagine a humid July afternoon. . . ." I circled my patient, reading from a script I had prepared; never having studied acting, I depended on my observation of TV detective dramas to give my performance validity and force . . . to hold the attention of Jesús Allendez—jaded watcher and apathetic consumer of such television fare.

"Two officers stand outside Mrs. Agatha Kent's apartment on the first floor of a brownstone in Washington Heights. Mrs. Kent's daughter, who lives in Canada, begins to worry when her mother neglects to call her at an appointed time. She asks the police to investigate. On entering the apartment they detect a foul odor. Someone's dead in there. On examining the premises it is determined that the apartment has also been ransacked. The daughter is needed to identify the DOA and to help the officers determine what, if anything, has been taken."

1

Those who scan the face for signals of inner intelligence may find it difficult to interpret the many fleeting expressions that appear upon it. I could not read Jesús's face. Either he did not recognize the story as having to do with him or the signals he emitted were too weak for me to pick up. I decided to expose him to other factual components of his history.

"Now, I want you to imagine a .32 caliber bullet . . . the cause of death."

"Should I shut my eyes?"

"If it helps you to imagine."

"Okay, they're shut."

I continued reading (in a tough voice) from the medical portion (abridged) of the court record: "This bullet, the .32 caliber messenger of death, takes the scenic route through Mrs. Kent's body. It gouges a pathway by entering the left upper abdomen; continues through the spleen, the diaphragm, and the left lung; forces itself into the base of the heart where the major blood vessel, called the inferior vena cava, brings all the blood up from the lower part of the body; then it rips through her right lung before exiting. The fire-arms expert not only confirms that this bullet is indeed a .32 caliber, but that it was fired from a weapon with a six-groove left-hand twist . . . probably a Colt firearm."

Jesús opened his eyes; smiled. "Man, you just like Quincy."

"Quincy?"

"The coroner on TV; he pick up these clues and takes 'em to his laboratory . . . cuts up dead people, like you just said. Now that's really somethin'."

My field of expertise is the criminal adolescent mind. The adolescent body does not interest me, and so it is not difficult at all to abstain from an intimacy that is sure to be disturbing to both patient and analyst. . . . I am a

2

professional with responsibility to a troubled clientele. In an early and highly regarded essay (popular within the mind-studies community), "Adolescent Flux in a Non-Ecstatic Environment," I stated that there is no need for the analysand to enter the analyst's body (or vice versa) since it is the closed mind one must attempt to open. In a later essay (not as easily accepted by my colleagues), "Participation Fantasies: A Further Exploration of the Primal-Scene Schema," I reversed my earlier position, and proposed that one must follow one's instincts in sexually provocative situations such as those that exist between patient and therapist: e.g., the documented sojourn of J. Posner (psychiatrist) who closeted himself for eight months with a delusional-venereal patient who finally removed the imaginary hand that rose from his left foot to a thoroughly aroused genital, and placed the doctor's hand there instead, thus curing himself; e.g., Kafka's country doctor who climbed into bed with a feverish patient in an attempt to draw the illness into himself; e.g., the revolutionary therapy of Dr. F. Thorpe who encouraged his profoundly regressed patient to weatherproof a drafty country cottage with her own defecation, thus allowing her to develop, after many an odoriferous month, into a useful member of society, an artist. These are the innovators who gave me the courage to continue with my own research; who demonstrated that there is more to process than cheese. However, as previously stated, it would be going against *my* instinct to have sex with a patient . . . there are other ways to be close.

When I first came into contact with Jesús Allendez, he was fifteen and a murderer. He had entered the apartment of a neighbor with the sole intention of robbing it; the neighbor returned home unexpectedly, found him rummaging among her belongings, and threatened to tell the police. After raping the woman, Jesús then shot her with her own gun. This surprised all who had known Jesús

3

and his family; however, his act was certainly psychologically logical: denial and repression as defense ... no emotional support available to him ... then complete mental and physical exhaustion till he "blew."

There were others who worked in Youth House who would have loved to get a crack at Jesús, to play with him in the name of science: the behaviorists with their electroconvulsive activity modification program (tempting and punishing, tempting and punishing till the subject could no longer be tempted); the chemotherapists offering a rainbow of pills that could induce benign mental absence in a violently present prisoner; the needle-M.D.s waiting with their sterile syringes for the time they would be called upon to create an imitation of death in the patient with their injections (augmented, of course, by shouted suggestions into the ears of the temporarily paralyzed patient, that he "be good"!). But I won out. We tossed a coin in the staff lunchroom, and Jesús was mine. At first I was authorized to see him only on weekend passes; later, when process and life became inseparable, Jesús moved in with me.

Before the first Allendez session I made myself some tea. I prepare it with morsels of lemon rind, strawberry preserves, tiny slices of sugared ginger, and a dash of dark rum. It is served in a glass held securely by a filigreed metal holder whose handle flares comically outward like a large ear. When I drink, it amuses me to hang onto this ear, sometimes pinching it. I do not lack a sense of humor.

The door to my office was left open purposely so that I could hear the stereo playing in the waiting room. I usually play chamber music of the string variety since it has a salutary effect on the anxieties of my patients. Brass, on the other hand, is liable to exacerbate an already excitable condition, though the use of brass is not contraindicated in cases where lethargy is the operative mode.

4

. . . However, I have noticed that when brass does rouse such patients, the activity is usually of the aimless type: a high-kneed trot around the magazine table, or the hideously automatic jerking of a head in time to, say, a Sousa trumpet solo. Even in the waiting room, one must pour oil on troubled waters.

If a patient is late to a session I do not take it lightly; the client arrives, carefully hiding his or her delight at having kept me waiting, or, as is more usual, the client arrives in almost total chagrin at having failed to live up to expectations. Immediately I make a terrible scene (I am human too), I throw myself on the floor, scream and cry out, yes, even pull at my hair (hoping it will not come out) in a ritual to show that I CARE. The patient may act in any of three ways:

1. Comfort me: this is GIVING.
2. Leave the vicinity: this is LEAVING.
3. Attack me: this is ATTACK RESPONSE.

I do not know how I would respond if attacked by a patient. . . . To find out, I would have to be put to the test. This frightens me.

Initially I was drawn to Jesús Allendez because of his babyish face: large brown eyes, prominent bulging forehead, and cowardly retreating chin. These juvenile features elicited strong feelings of affection from me. He resembled Mickey Mouse, my favorite childhood comic character (I wear a Mickey Mouse watch, and drink from a souvenir Mickey Mouse tumbler). I still admire Mickey for his loyalty to a number of creatures: his lady-love Minnie, a horse called Horace, and a dog Pluto. He is marvelously multitalented, having been a sea captain, an orchestra conductor, a car salesman, and a sorcerer's apprentice . . . altogether a healthy role-model, and a totally integrated personality. One would not expect to find Mickey

5

in an analyst's office, though I am sure there were times he could not cope . . . times he suffered from guilt . . . times he thought of himself as a bad guy.

The tea had just begun to cool when Jesús entered the study. He was uncomfortable and stood at the door waiting for a summons from me.

"You may sit right there," I said, indicating the chair opposite me. I offered him a candy from the bowl of sweets I keep on my desk. He took a Hopje, that delicious coffee-flavored candy imported from Holland, the land of windmills. . . . Opposite Jesús Allendez, I, like Don Quixote's innocent windmills, would have to prove myself friend not foe.

"You've made a good choice," I remarked, but he was so involved in obtaining oral satisfaction from the confection that he ignored my friendly, ego-boosting attempt. "They're a favorite of mine too."

His legs were pressed together, knees thrust against my desk, an uncomfortable position, but a safe one: when the body hurts, the body exists. Raissa, my police dog, lay near the window on an antique blue-and-gold Kirman rug. Generally Raissa is gentle and affectionate, but who knows. . . . Before allowing her to remain in the consulting room I had considered what my patients might think about such a large and possibly dangerous dog being present. I had also considered that the beast's attendance might reinforce a fear of losing control in my patients. Wasn't the dog there to protect ME from THEM? At any rate, Raissa would not have been happy in another room away from me.

"Tastes like coffee," Jesús said finally.

"Have another."

He took another candy but did not unwrap it, and put it into his pocket. "For later," he explained.

"Do you know why you're here?" I asked.

"Counselor says you wanna see what makes me tick."

6

"Not completely true. I want to help you."

"Okay with me." He slumped in the chair, demonstrating that it would be very difficult indeed to straighten him out.

"I understand you're a TV watcher . . ."

"Used to be before . . ."

"Before?"

"Before I got in trouble."

"What kind of trouble?"

"You know . . ."

"Mrs. Kent?"

"Yeah."

"Does it bother you that you killed her?"

"It bother me when I first kill her, but the more I don't think about it, the more it don't bother me."

"But it still bothers you a little?"

"Yeah, it do."

"Anything in particular about it?"

"Maybe it what I ate . . . I didn' feel so good."

"What you ate?"

"On the day that it happen I was in Kentucky Fried Chicken . . . the chicken is nice and extra crispy there . . . I like the drumstick best . . . but it more expensive by the piece . . . the potato salad and the coleslaw is extra . . . they got strawberry shortcake in them little plastic cups they call buckets . . . and let me tell you, man, it taste better than the apple pie at Burger King . . . only two pieces of apple in there . . . Kentucky Fried Chicken got its bad points too . . . when you first walk in it smell like throw-up . . . that the cookin' oil . . . when you leave the smell is in your clothes, and hair, and it ain't no secret where you been."

This nitpicking truthfulness, this nauseating embroidery that purported to be an answer to my question, was an obvious evasion by Jesús of material too hot to handle. I was led to believe that I was dealing with a prime exam-

7

ple of the obsessive-compulsive personality dangerously bordering on schizophrenia: a self-defense system easily aggravated by the culinary promise of cheap food chains.

One might argue that most therapists do not love an obsessive, and ask, "Why are you, Mathilda Brody, bothering with Jesús Allendez?" At the moment I have no answer. It is the same as when I first developed a passion for African violets.

I could hardly have known, when I received a free plant at a flower show I attended many years ago, that an exhilarating affair was about to begin. The gift plant was, of course, an African violet. I was afraid that it would not live, that my "green" thumb was not the green of life but the purulence of death. However, I became determined that it would survive, and ministered to it. In time the plant bloomed. Many enjoyable years of African violet involvement ensued.

Caring for the "most commonly grown houseplant in the world" gave me peace of mind, it was such a "mindless" occupation. I knew what was required. I did not have to ask questions. Blankets of colorful flowers became my security blanket . . . I was transfixed by rosettes of velvety leaves; my sensual nature satisfied. Only someone dead to the beauty of plants could bring just one African violet into bloom without wanting more. . . . I began collecting this charismatic plant.

They flowered off and on all year long, took up little space (a profusion of pots gathered where some direct sunlight might shine, or a bit of reflected light), kept healthy and contented without a great deal of fuss and bother. Single, semidouble, fringed or ruffled, in varying shades of blue, pink, lavender, wine, purple, and white, I loved them all, and had no favorites. Their environment was kept pleasantly moist and warm (since the African in African violet is a clue to their care). I learned to doctor my plants, to rid them of the cottony mealybug who causes a fuzzy, white fungus to invade the heart of the plant. Weekly I would use a magnifying glass to inspect them.

A few months ago the affair ended as suddenly as it had begun. I gave my plants away to other tenants in the building. As a final snub to my past mania I purchased a large artificial philodendron whose shiny green leaves needed only to be touched with a damp cloth every three days to remove dust. It has always been my policy to stop while I am ahead. I had gone as far as I could go with the African violets: turned my back on them before they could betray me (living things wilt and die on one, no matter how much devotion is put into their care . . . failure preordained). Though I could never hope to love the fake philodendron, it would never cause me grief. And at a distance it was pretty, it was shiny, it was green.

"Where did you go after you left Kentucky Fried Chicken?"

Jesús put one fat finger into his nostril, a displacement from down (the genital) to up. It does not work the opposite way. A nose picker is a small-time masturbator, but a masturbator is not necessarily a nose picker. A nose picker is also a collector; many nose pickers become archeologists when other avenues of endeavor are closed to them. Excavation yields many things that are not objects of beauty: broken bits of things (fecal sculpture), fossilized spheres (beads of snot), etc. Therefore Jesús was not merely clearing a passageway, he was practicing pocket pool with a surrogate (pool) cue.

"If you take your finger out of your nose you'll be able to answer me," I said, knowing full well what I was forbidding him to do.

"Don't have nothin' to say," my patient said.

I keep an X-Acto knife in my desk drawer. It is razor-sharp and can whittle wood or flesh to a fine point. On an impulse I cut into my thumb, drawing blood. My hand returned to the top of the desk in full view of the patient. This self-inflicted stigma was intended as a goad to Jesús's phlegmatic attitude toward me, but I had miscalculated . . . he did not react. After carefully encircling the tip of my finger with a flesh-colored Band-Aid, I said, "I bled for you, and my name isn't even Jesus."

This opened the floodgates; he talked.

"Mom sure made a mistake when she name me Jesús . . . ain't no resemblance . . . Jesús he save the whores; I fuck 'em . . . Jesús he bring the dead back to life; I kill 'em. . . . How old you think Jesús was when he kiss his mom goodbye? My age? You know, Jesús take after his mom. She did the first miracle when she make the immaculate conception, then he went and cure the leper, walk on the water, and like that. The nuns in school was mad at me for being the wrong Jesús. They was waitin' for the other one."

"There are miracles, and there are miracles," I said.

"What you sayin'?"

"That someday you'll perform your own miracle."

"Bullshit!"

"Wait and see."

"Sure . . . sure."

"Would it make you happy if you could?"

"Wanna know what I think happiness is?"

"Yes."

"Happiness is punching your sister. Happiness is shooting your mother. Happiness is stabbing your father. Happiness is exploding the world. That the kind of miracle make me happy." He looked at me smugly, hoping he had shocked me.

"That's the kind of miracle that got you in the mess you're in right now," I said.

"No shit?"

"What do you think?"

10

"You don't want me to say the truth. You like the teachers in school what put me down."

"If you like the truth so much why don't you tell me what you did when you left Kentucky Fried Chicken?"

"Didn' do nothin'."

"Nothing?"

"Nothin' important."

"It's important enough for you to keep quiet about. . . . What are you hiding from me, Jesús?"

"Nothin' . . . I just went in there."

"In where?"

"The old lady's house."

"Agatha Kent's apartment?"

"I was lookin' for the money she hid there. She came in and started to yell, so I made her stop."

"How?"

"Covered her mouth. She bit me. Made me mad."

"So you raped her?"

"You know."

"And shot her?"

"That the way it happen. It sure surprise me. I thought she was fakin' when she wouldn' get up."

"So you left her there?"

"Yeah, I did."

"But you took your time."

"Gettin' out?"

"Yes."

"Well, I accomplished my mission."

"What mission?"

"To get what I came for, you know."

"The money?"

"Yeah."

"The TV?"

"Yeah."

"The gun?"

"Whatdya think?"

11

"I think you took off."

"I got into the old lady's car. The seat was still warm, and I went to my friend Henley. Solly Rodriguez was there too, and we agree to go partyin'. We got the money and all. Solly pulls out his lousy four dollars. Henley has eight. I uncurl the money from Mrs. Kent's . . . 'bout five hundred dollars on the table."

"Your friends must have been impressed."

"Shit in their pants . . . I told them I won it at craps. Not that they care where it come from. Then I say I got a gun. They was hot to see it . . . I open the trunk of the car. It look like there ain't nothin' in it except a dirty old rag and a blanket . . . but the gun is in the rag. . . . Man, it knock them out to see that snub-nose baby! Solly says, 'Hey look, there's only five shells, what'd you do with the other one?' He know about guns all right. I say I shot a rat with it. Then I go around to where Henley is and I point the gun at his head. 'There's a lot more rats to shoot,' I say laughin'. He put his hands up like this. . . . He's shakin' and yellin', 'Don't, don't!' He think I really gonna do it. No way! He's my buddy. On the way to Coney Island a cop stop us for speedin' . . . I mean Henley got a license so the cop give him a ticket, then he let us go. It was a close call."

"How was it a close call?"

"If we was arrested right there I wouldn't have went to Coney Island, do the rides and all."

"No."

"You know, we stay there awhile, then we went to the motel and I fell asleep. So then I was sleeping, and Solly woke me up and said there was girls in the room, to wake up."

"Did you wake up?"

"Yeah, so I said, fine, I woke up. Then we just stayed with them like around that time in the morning they left, and we went to sleep."

"You were acting like all the other fellows, right?"

12

"Right."

"You killed a woman, you were driving in a stolen car, you were given a ticket for speeding, you threatened a friend with a gun, you spent stolen money on amusement park rides, there were girls in your room till the wee hours of the morning, and you slept good after all of that. . . . Is this the normal conduct of boys your age?"

"As far as I know, Doc."

As far as *anyone* knows there is no norm. Perhaps the sociopath is normal since *his* sociopathic act causes *him* no grief. In this society the individual expects happiness as *his* birthright. To be guilty, to feel remorse, to experience grief, is a symptom; is not the acceptable mode, and must be denied. Thus, the sociopath does not suffer, or has suffered in the past to no avail; *he* commits *his* (affectless) criminal act as a concession to society. Did this mean that Jesús was well? Was I mad trying to "cure" a well man?

A valid diagnostic tool is the interpretation of a patient's art . . . to this end I provided Jesús with art materials. He promptly involved himself in patterning (repetition) and the sketching in of an unimaginative collection of lines and color (using the lines to trap the color). His efforts reminded me of a net thrown over a struggling beast to keep it within safe bounds; not a color bled beyond its prison. Given more time, he spent it correcting and erasing what he had already done, unable to finish one picture to his satisfaction. The process was a denial of creativity, duplicating the manner in which he had lived his life. When I substituted fingerpaints, hoping that the gloppy consistency would permit Jesús to muck around freely, he refused to play. "It's baby shit!" was his comment. And he was right.

"What exactly is your objection to baby shit?" I asked.

"I got better things to do," he answered.

13

"Name some."

"Fuck you."

"Fuck you, too."

"Hey, you're not supposed to talk that way, Doc!"

"Why not?"

"It ain't nice."

"Then why do you talk that way?"

"That's the way I always talk."

My use of language to create a camaraderie between us made Jesús uncomfortable. I was not his peer, and I was a female. Nice women—his mother, TV anchorwomen, the President's wife—did not speak that way. Even his victim, Mrs. Kent, did not speak that way.

"Do you mind if I talk to your mother before I see you again?"

"Why you wanna bother her?"

"I need some additional background concerning you ... nothing secret ... it'll be on tape. You'll be able to hear it if you want to."

"No skin, Doc ... go ahead. It your business. You just do what you hafta do."

# 2

That evening I left a message for Mrs. Allendez with someone in the Allendez household, and was waiting for her to call me back. When the phone rang, the voice on the line was shaky and high-pitched: a young woman in distress; not Mrs. Allendez.

"Dr. Brody?"

"Speaking."

"I saw your name in the paper, you're the analyst who . . ."

"Who are you, please? Who am I speaking with?"

"This is Allison Kent. My mother was Agatha Kent, that's who!"

"Yes? What can I do for you?"

"You can stop treating that little pig Jesús Allendez with kid gloves. He deserves to be shot in the street like a dog!"

I took umbrage at the dog remark . . . dogs do not deserve an impromptu execution, unless, running wild in the streets with rabies, they threaten human beings. I remembered *The Story of Louis Pasteur,* seen during one of its revivals on TV . . . a child screaming while the bite was being cauterized.

"Miss Kent, please! I know it's an emotional issue."

"You bet it is!"

"Would you like to make an appointment to see me?" I glanced at my watch. It was getting late and my dinner date would be trying to reach me.

"I don't want to see you," Allison Kent said. Her voice tickled my eardrum and sent prickly vibrations down my throat.

"Then I'm afraid I have to cut our conversation short. I'm expecting other calls."

"Bullshit, Dr. Brody!"

The suddenness of this vulgarity surprised me. "Miss Kent, I've been hearing that word a lot lately and I don't like it."

She began to cry softly. "What about the victim? What about me?"

"I can see you this evening if you'd like. How about after ten?"

"Okay," Miss Kent agreed, "about a quarter after."

Promptly at ten, Allison Kent arrived at my door. She was a very tall woman, possibly six feet tall, unkempt (her dress looked as if she had slept in it. Her hair fell over her face in oily strands), yet she was good-looking in a raw-boned, energetic way. She held in her hand an old-fashioned, handle-at-the-top briefcase that she set carefully beside her on the floor when she sat down. I sensed that the flat, rectangular case held something of value to Miss Kent. Noticing Raissa, she called to her, but Raissa refused to leave her rug to be petted. I used to believe that animals were the best judge of people, immediately ferreting out the bad (barking them into a corner, or chewing them to death), or singling out the good (with a friendly wagging tail, or a warm, wet tongue), but Raissa's mood, more

16

often than not, depended on her doggy dreams, when she had eaten, and whether her corner was warm. No doubt, Raissa was far too comfortable to move when Miss Kent tried to get her attention.

"I've brought something you might be interested in," she said, taking some sheets of paper out of the briefcase. "Momma wrote this a few days before she was murdered."

I took the pages and laid them on the desk. "Do you want me to read them now, or may I keep them for a while?"

"I have copies," she answered. "I always make copies of everything. Things disappear . . . sometimes forever; I found that out!"

"Exactly! So, I'll hold onto these."

"Keep them as long as you like."

"All right."

"People say I'm a duplicate of Mother. I'm not."

"You're the original?"

"I'm completely different."

"How?"

"I'm not superstitious; I'm not old; I'm not kind; and I'm tall. She was far from tall. She was limber but she wasn't tall. Of course, our eyes were the same color but we saw things differently, and our noses adored smelling roses. . . . Other than that, no resemblance."

"Would you care for a candy?"

She recoiled in horror. "My teeth would fall out!"

I recognized a health faddist, and withdrew the offer. "I apologize for offering you what must be in your opinion a gift of poison."

"I have to take care of myself; I'm the only one left," she explained. "There was only Mother and me. I brush my teeth with French clay and table salt. I never eat sweets."

"The Kleenex is here on the desk," I pointed out, "if

17

you need some." I sensed that it was about to be crying time for Allison Kent, innocuous though the subject of tooth decay was.

"It's in a pretty box. It's pretty enough to put in a guest room, or the foyer, or the bathroom, or anywhere a person might sneeze, or cry," Allison sobbed, dabbing the wet flesh below her eyes. "Momma kept the box with pink flowers in the bedroom, and the one with the silver stripes in the kitchen. . . . Ohhhh, when I lost Momma I lost everything . . . couldn't sleep, couldn't eat, lost my job . . . everything, everything."

"Not everything."

"Mother deserved better than what she got."

"Yes."

"She even befriended that boy. The one who killed her. They used to talk about TV. She liked the interview shows, the game shows, the soaps. . . . Well, we know what he liked! When do you see him? I'd like to confront him . . . I'd like to see him cringe."

"That's not advisable, Miss Kent. It would serve no purpose."

"It would make me feel better."

"Not necessarily. Your mother . . ."

"My mother?"

"Was a generous person?"

"She was generous to a fault; that was her downfall."

What does "generous to a fault" mean? If generosity is a quality, how can one be too generous? Obviously, there can be too much of a good thing, and that is *bad.* It would be impossible to be stingy to a fault, since being stingy is already a fault (bad). Another question I had for myself. Why is the word "downfall" and not "falldown"? Is the *direction* more important than the action? The questions I asked myself during the Allison Kent session took me in a direction away from her. . . . It was late, I was tired, and wanted to escape.

18

Allison said, "I'm still angry at that Jesús . . . I don't understand why you want to help that low-life scum! Who cares *why* he did it! The fact that he *did* it should qualify him for perpetual punishment, if not death by firing squad, hanging, cyanide pellet, and the electric chair!"

"I'm a scientist, Allison, not an executioner . . . for all I know, Jesús has one of those elusive and wonderfully complicated double, triple, or quadruple personalities. I've never had a case like that. It doesn't mean that on a human level I don't despise the frightful little murderer. It doesn't mean that I don't sympathize with you. It doesn't even mean that I'm not fearful for my own life and wonder what the world's coming to . . ."

"Then what does it mean?" Allison implored.

"It means that your mother is a memory and nothing more can be done for her; however, the sick mind that committed her murder can be parted like the Red Sea and crossed. I propose to make this journey as an impartial observer, leading my theories and intuitive non sequiturs to safety across the upper and lower quadrants of experience."

"You've never lost anyone you loved," Allison concluded unfairly, "or you wouldn't be so cold."

I did not argue with her since my personal life had no bearing on her analysis; however, I had lost my own mother in the immutable past: she had had to be hacked out of a sheet of ice where she had been found, under a broken waterpipe, in our tiny apartment during a fuel shortage. I had been farmed out to an aunt who received heat, and so was saved; nothing I could do would bring my mother back to me. The coldness Allison accused me of was the unencumbered clarity of my desire to know and to examine evil . . . to recognize its incipient stages without prejudice, and to record it for posterity (in the great library of knowledge), after which, who knows, some of it might prove useful.

19

On her way out, Allison promised me she would go right home, take two dolomite tablets and a vitamin B₆, then pop right into bed—"Relaxes me," she explained. "I prefer to self-medicate . . . I trust myself."

Her trust in herself was certainly misplaced.

"The *saucissons en croûte* were delightful," Harry mumbled as I got into bed. "I'll never forget the crust, the moist lining, the stuffing . . . mmmmm. . . . What's in the refrigerator?"

"You've had enough to eat, darling, go to sleep," I said.

"Don't you want to make love?"

"I've got work to do . . . pages and pages to write before I rest."

"Look at what I've got for you." He untied his pajama bottoms. An erection in its initial stages had begun its wary climb to local fame. "Take a bow for the lady," Harry said, and the genital stirred in my direction.

I gave it a gentle kiss. "When did you learn that trick?"

"Kiss me again, and I won't bother you for the rest of the evening," Harry said. "It feels so good."

The first time I saw Harry naked was in a summer cottage (oceanfront) near Provincetown. I had not yet begun my practice, and was vacationing with mutual friends. We had decided to go swimming; my friends, a married couple, went into the bedroom to change into swimsuits; Harry and I were left in the living room, where he disrobed. His body was round and pale, enlivened only by a cicatrix about six inches long on the left buttock.

"How did you get that?" I asked. The scar was raised; perfectly healed; it had been made years before.

"An unfriendly encounter," he answered. "You wouldn't be interested."

"You can't just show me that thing and not tell me about it!" I insisted.

"I'll bet you want to touch it too . . . go ahead." He stood waiting.

"Why would I want to touch it?" I glanced at the bedroom door, behind which our friends were dressing, wondering if they were about to come out.

"I've been told it's an exciting thing to do . . . like touring the scene of a crime," Harry said.

"Someone cut you there?" I observed the scar, though still at a distance.

"Someone put his initials there with a Swiss pocket-knife . . . I never dreamed his logo would become a turn-on for new lovers. . . . Come on, touch it. Close your eyes if you have to." He drew me to him and placed my fingers on the knotty raised skin.

"Braille of the flesh," I commented, my eyes closed. "The story I am reading with my fingertips is a sad, sad story."

"Do you like men?" Harry asked.

"Yes, I do," I answered, "but not exclusively."

"Me too."

"Did it hurt terribly?"

"Liking both men and women?"

"No, the cut . . . did you cry out?"

"I was gagged and couldn't make a sound. The knife was very sharp and it hurt like hell. He took his time too, watching me squirm while his friend held me down. Imagine, cutting his initials into me as if I were a tree. I've been to every gay bar in New York for the last five years looking for him . . . I want to thank him."

"Thank him? For what?"

"For giving me a cachet."

"You don't mean that!" I said, shocked.

"Don't I! However, the one thing I can't forgive him for is where it happened . . . at home in ordinary surround-

21

ings, among my plants, books, and records. That was ruthless. We were having what I thought was a charming evening together: cocktails, dinner, music, things one does to increase the normality of a strained relationship, when suddenly Harper—that's his name—dropped his plate on the floor, then left, ostensibly to go to the kitchen, but instead let in his cohort. One moment complete relaxation and trust, the next a shocking violation."

Later that day, I was told by my friends, who had been listening to Harry through the bedroom door, that Harry loved to make up horror stories, and would say anything to dramatize himself.

Alone in the car with me, on our way home from the beach, Harry asked to make love . . . actually he'd asked if he could *try* to make love to me. I told him that I did not allow people to practice on me, but that when he had perfected both his desire and his technique, I would be available. He amused me, and I was curious about him. Before the end of the month we became imperfect lovers (since perfection is always out of reach, and the clumsy, fallible lover has his charms too), able to perform infrequently without inhibition.

Around that time, Harry's only claim to fame was his reputation for daring: he had appeared in a number of early "happenings" dressed as an angel and smoking a cigar. Much later he starred in a movie sitting in a rocking chair smoking a cigar. By the time he had grown a prematurely gray beard, he had been painted by a British artist, seated on a couch before a window, smoking a cigar. What distressed him most about the Cuban revolution was the difficulty it caused him in getting Havana cigars. He loved to play his vintage Fanny Brice records for me, and bought me Art Deco cigarette holders, since at that time I was a heavy smoker. His smoking jacket was authentic circa 1890: burgundy velvet with quilted satin lapels. He lived for a while on Central Park West, not far from where

I am now, and then farther downtown, a few blocks from Carnegie Hall.

For three years Harry languished in the West Fifties, and worked at the New Metropolitan Museum as one of their curators. He told me he had been hired because of his special taste in art: this had progressed from kitsch backward to Early American, skipped to Pop, embraced Op, welcomed the energetic "experimental," and rejoiced when "bad" art came into its own. "I know when something's good," he boasted to me. "I get nauseous; when I'm nauseous I'm sure." The first show he curated made him very nauseous. The critics and the public got sick too: they were sure the show was lousy, that Harry had only included the work of close friends. "It's strictly my taste, and not an example of all the good work done in the last decade," he'd replied. "I'm sorry if I didn't include people other people consider important. That would be someone else's show and someone else's taste, not mine!"

He was always amazed to find me in the kitchen. "My father never allowed my mother into the kitchen; she didn't even know where it was," he said. It was then that I found out Harry's family owned diamond mines, and that he was an heir. With others he played the young esthete who makes it on wits alone. I had suspected he was different when, eating out at Jamais Toujours, he sent back three bottles of wine that were not to his liking.

"What are you reading?" Harry asked, snuggling closer.

"God, Harry, what do you want?"

"I want more! Give me your mouth, your hand, your inner thighs . . . whatever you can spare. I'm a man in need."

"How about my feet? I'm using my hands already."

"Are they clean?" the fastidious Harry inquired. He was not needy enough to throw caution to the winds.

"As clean as clean can be," I replied truthfully, having scrubbed, rubbed, and pedicured my feet that very evening.

I have a special affection for my feet, so often mistreated and ignored, the scapegoats of the body.

"Your feet will do," he agreed with no trace of humor, bringing himself, genitally speaking, closer to my feet. His penis felt warm and wobbly; ineffectual would have been Harry's word for it, but to me, the uninvolved outsider, it was charming, nonthreatening, and natural. Detumescence should never be thought of as feeble; it is the place where tumescence can occur.

Harry was a nuisance; he could not just go to sleep . . . the arms of Morpheus were a frightening place to be, one might never wake up. Harry had to be knocked out with an orgasm; he would not go quietly. It was this habit of his that more and more often made me consider ending the relationship in its present form, and perhaps seeing him on a nonsexual basis. He was an excellent sounding board on questions of moment. I needed him for that. Meanwhile, I tolerated his intrusive masturbatory rhythm while reading Mrs. Agatha Kent's papers.

## KENT FILE

### PRIVATE PAPERS OF AGATHA KENT

I went to bed later than usual because I wanted to see the "Tomorrow" show. They had circus freaks. There was the Baby-Woman who was half-woman/half-baby. She must have been about sixty years old, and there wasn't any part of her a baby any more, but she was sitting in a chair so I didn't get to see the bottom part of her. It was hidden under a big skirt. There was a fire-swallowing midget called the Tongue of Iron. The host made an off-color remark about how the Tongue of Iron must be popular with

24

the ladies. There was a sad-looking sword swallower, very sad-looking indeed. He put a sword right down his throat and then another sword that had a gun at the top. When he swallowed the whole sword, he shot the gun. The sound made me jump. What a surprise. His teeth must have rattled. I don't feel sorry for those people, not even the sad-looking one, because they're still out in the world and getting paid for it, while I'm retired and trying to make ends meet on very little. I should have stayed a dancer, but settled for teacher. In a dancer the legs wear out fast, and that's why I stopped. Well, dear diary, after all the excitement I went to bed later than usual, as I mentioned before. I tossed and turned, but finally did fall asleep, and had this dream. In the dream there was a deathlike stillness around me. I wondered whether I could move through it. Then I heard sobs, as if an entire audience were weeping on cue. The weeping would start and stop suddenly. In the dream I left my bed and went into another room. I could still hear sobbing but the mourners were invisible. I went from room to room searching for them. The house was brightly lit, unlike me to leave the lights on, well, dear, every object stood out in the bright light, and every object was familiar: the cut-glass collection, the Hummel figurines, the black lacquered box with mother-of-pearl inlay, the Japanese prints, the hand-crocheted pillows. Still the sound of grieving filled the room. I was determined to discover the meaning of this immense sorrow. In the dream I went into the parlor and there I met with a sickening surprise. On my beautiful Bechstein grand piano rested an ornate coffin, the expensive kind with brass fittings, and lined in chartreuse velvet. Its sides were draped with refundable food coupons attached to paper napkins made of two-ply tissue. One of these napkins was tucked under the chin of the corpse. A throng of people, elevated about a foot off the floor, were gazing mournfully at the corpse and digging at it with my best silver. Occasionally a member of the group would pry open the mouth of the dead person and force it to eat. I asked the dream-person, "Who is the dead person you are trying to feed?" The horrifying answer came,

"Mrs. Agatha· Kent." "But I'm alive," I insisted. The dream-person said, "If you wish to corroborate the story, consult the END OF JOURNEY section of your newspaper." "How did I meet my end?" I asked. "She was murdered by a youthful assassin," the dream-person wailed. I woke from my nightmare drenched in sweat. Though it was only a dream, dear, dear diary, I've been preoccupied by it ever since.

So, Mrs. Agatha Kent had had precognition, just as Abraham Lincoln had, but in each case it had done them no good; not once had I been able to predict the future (a hideous gift). It is not as hideous to try to alter the future through analysis; this too is a gift. I resisted altering Mrs. Kent's diary, a compulsion I have whenever new material comes to me for my file. . . . The method I have evolved for reading between the lines is writing between the lines: newspaper clippings, suicide notes, shopping lists, announcements, requests for contributions, letters, have all been changed by me so as to extract a deeper meaning, or to emphasize the absurd side of life. Just because a column, an article, an obituary has been published does not mean that the information it contains is correct . . . or complete. Neither is any human being completed, fortunately. If I were to accept things at face value, what would there be for me to do? And what hope for others?

# 3

My first appointment was at nine. Harry left at eight-thirty. I didn't like having him around after that; there was always the possibility that he would be seen by a patient. Only once had any patient met Harry, and that was accidental. There had been a fire in the tenants' elevator, service was halted and the rear elevator pressed into use. Harry was going down and a patient was coming up. Just as the door opened on my floor (the third) Harry kissed me, and we were seen. For weeks this material came up in the patient's analysis. He became so jealous (replacing, in his mind, his father for Harry, his mother for me) that violence threatened to erupt. This was during the time that Raissa was away at Dr. Kohlmar's after a serious mishap with a car. Without her protection I had to refer the dangerous patient to another analyst. Harry's kisses seldom came to happy conclusions.

Nina Allendez was a stout, solidly built woman in her late thirties. She truly cared for her son and was eager to offer whatever help she could.

"I was just a kid myself when I had him . . . the guy who was the father, well, he didn't want to marry me . . . couldn't is more like it . . . he wasn't more than eighteen himself . . . out of a job . . . living at home. When I told him I was pregnant he disappeared . . . so I had the baby and saw there wasn't any future for us in Puerto Rico . . . I couldn't get a job neither . . . maybe I coulda in one of them big tourist hotels . . . but bein' a maid wasn't my idea of livin', you know, not then. So I took a trip to the States and left the boy with his grandmother who loved him. Always I was thinkin' about the boy and how was he doing. I wanted a better life for us. So, I met this guy Al and we got married. I didn't know he'd be so damn strict with the kid. I sent for Jesús when he was five. He couldn't speak American, only Spanish. The way he learned English actually was by watching the TV."

"How much TV did he watch?"

"He watched from the time he got up in the morning till he went to sleep. From the time he got here in April and he didn't have to go to school till September. Al thought it was great because the kid didn't get in his hair. He didn't show him affection or nothin'. Only thing he complained about was what the electricity cost. Bitchin' at me."

"So, whose idea was it, about television as a way to teach Jesús English?"

"There was nothin' else he could do. I had to work. Al had to work. We found this old lady to come and keep an eye on Jesús. He was very active. I was afraid he'd run away. He was a very trusting kid, you know, and would open the door to let anybody in the apartment. So the TV was good. And for him it was wonderful because he never saw a TV till he came here."

"Do you remember the first words he learned?"

"He ran around like crazy yelling, 'Bang! Bang!' playing cops and robbers. Pretty soon the old lady couldn't stand it."

"Did there come a time when he began to imitate more of the things he saw on TV?"

"He fell in love with them 'Superman' reruns, and he asked me to open the window so he could jump out and try to fly. I told him it was a TV trick, but when we went to Coney Island, to the beach, he used to take a plastic bag like you get at the A&P for storing leaky food, and he'd wrap the bag around his neck, and the air went in the bag, and gave him like . . . ?"

"Wings?"

"Yeah, like wings. Then he used to run back and forth. I took pictures of him doing that. I tried to stop him, but he wouldn't let me. He was always trying to rescue someone."

"Like Superman?"

"Yes. He really thought he was Superman. But sometimes I'd have to tie him up. I was always careful to tie him loose, you know, I didn't like to do it."

"Did Jesús graduate from elementary school?"

"Yeah, but I had to take him out for a while in fifth grade, from the Catholic school. The nuns didn't want to deal with him because of his behavior."

"What did they object to?"

"Oh . . . he would, he got into arguments with the nuns about sitting still in class and about not doing his homework. He got 'em real mad when he talked about how Superman would have rescued Christ off the Cross faster than the speed of light."

"Did you have to visit the school?"

"Yes, I was in school whenever they called me, and they told me that he was too active . . . they couldn't keep him."

"Then what?"

"So they asked me to place him in another school, so

29

I did. He went to public school and for a year he did pretty good."

"What year was that?"

"Sixth grade."

"And how old was Jesús by that time?"

"Let me see . . . eleven? Eleven years old . . . but he looked younger. He didn't grow fast like the other kids. He's still kind of small for his age."

"What were his television habits by this time? Was he starting to watch different kinds of programs, other than 'Superman'?"

"He knew every single thing that was on TV . . . the neighborhood expert, I called him. . . . I don't watch too much TV myself."

"Did you know what he was watching?"

"He'd want me to sit with him and watch, but Al got angry and told me not to be so soft and do everything the kid wanted. Then Jesús would tell me about his programs. He loved the scary movies, which I hate. He'd make me annoyed by the plots, you know, crazy people following innocent victims, stabbing, shooting, like that. He liked the police movies and could talk about them very well. I swear I thought he was a professor of TV . . . not going to be a killer himself."

"Why did you allow him to watch these programs that you did not approve of?"

"I didn't allow him."

"Then how did it happen?"

"Well, I used to lay down about eight o'clock because I had to get up at ten-thirty to go to work."

"You mean at night?"

"Yes."

"What is it you work at, Mrs. Allendez?"

"I'm on the housekeeping staff at 30 Rockefeller Plaza."

"Not too much traffic at that time . . ."

"I go on the subway . . . it's slow . . . wait and wait for a train, always be scared someone's gonna come along and push me on the track. But it's nice and quiet where I work . . . no one bothers me."

"Well, the city's a war zone, isn't it, Mrs. Allendez?"

"What can we do?"

"Just what you're doing . . . going about your business. . . . Now, what about your son's daily habits?"

"Lonely, very lonely. Last year I registered him in the after-school program. They had basketball, softball, swimming . . . things like that, so I thought it would be a good place for him to get away from the TV, but we got his report card and it was bad. So my husband and me, well, we decided he should stay out of the center as punishment. He didn't want to do his homework, he didn't want to read . . . not even the comics. He just, he would only watch TV. Couple of times Al would catch him good with the strap, or not let him eat with us. Nothing worked. And I was going crazy. I love my son, but I swear I felt like killing him. He was the main problem I was thinking about."

"Did Jesús have any other problems, personal problems that caused you to worry?"

"What you mean by personal, Dr. Brody?"

"A problem not having to do with school or TV."

"Yeah, he did somethin' that was a problem for both of us; he wouldn't stop wettin' his bed. I didn't need the extra work. . . . First thing when I got in from my job, I'd have to change the kid's sheets. Even the mattress stunk. We bought a rubber sheet that went under the regular sheet but he threw it on the floor. Said it smelled funny and made him sweat. At first I used to wake him up at night to get him to go to the toilet . . . but then I got the night job. What makes a kid that old go in bed?"

"Could be a lot of things."

"Yeah? What?"

"Could be physical . . . or psychological."

"Yeah, but whose fault is it? Al blames me."

"Mrs. Allendez, no one may be at fault."

"Well, that's good for a change."

"Are you feeling guilty?"

"He's my kid and look at what happened. I never should have left him so long. I should have taken him with me to New York."

"Would you like a Kleenex?"

"Thanks . . . I cry a lot lately . . . I never know when I'm gonna cry. . . ."

"I understand."

"Do you have a bathroom . . . I mean, could I use . . ."

"Go back out to the hall where you came in, then turn left. It's the first door on the right."

My thoughts on bed-wetting were ordinary ones, not up to the brilliant conclusions I had reached on other matters pertaining to the psychology of the child, the adolescent, and the postadolescent (a.k.a. the adult). Thought 1: A warm bed is a desirable bridge or souvenir from infancy. The temperature, the smell, the comfort trigger memories of a more secure time. Thought 2: By wetting the bed (relinquishing control) the bed-wetter feels physical relief and at the same time gets the attention he craves. He is also punishing the mother. She does not react with love. She hurts him. It is attention, nevertheless, and he translates it as love. Thought 3: The urine finds its way out of the genital. Thus the bed-wetter calls attention to his genital. There is incestuous intent in this activity. The mother (subconsciously) understands this, and must reject the son's sexual overtures. A further complication is the situation of stepfather (interloper): a triumvirate of mother, son, and stepfather creates a tense, untenable situation. Bed-wetting is a sport the child enters into competitively to displace the stepfather in the affections of the mother. He experiences guilt (oedipal).

I played with the idea of placing pots of urine (hidden behind the couch, under the desk, on a bookshelf) around the room during the next Jesús Allendez session. If Proust's lemon-flavored pastries could release memory, why not the fragrance of piss?

NOTE: Night-wetting is related to helplessness and anger.

Mrs. Allendez, composed and dry-eyed, returned to sit on the couch beside me.

"Jesús wanted Al to shave his head like Kojak."

"Did he do it?"

"Almost. Then he didn't. Jesús was upset."

"Why do you think he wanted your husband to do that?"

"I don't know. Maybe it would help him to like Al. I don't know."

"He liked Kojak?"

"He liked him better than people."

"Did Jesús ever run away from home?"

"Sure. One Saturday he got a beating from Al because of his report card from school. That week was very bad. All the teachers said that they couldn't do nothing with Jesús. He wasn't listening or doing his homework . . . and he left this letter."

*Dear Mom,*

*Each day that goes by I get more and more depresd with life. You know that I am caged up like an animal ever since I come home and stay with you and Al. I know that you didn ever want me back with you two. You made me the way I am now just a shell of a person who once was. I'm just a bum now and I always will be. When I was little I*

33

*was just like Superman, in my heart I want to be good, but there nothing left of me any more. I'm cracking. Maybe I have a chance if you leave Al who hate me. But you wont leave him. So be watching someday for a call from the police saying Mrs. Allendez we are sory to infom you of your sons arrest, would you please come down to the staton house to idenfy him. Hes kind of mangeled up because we had a shootout and shot his arms and legs. We had to use a M-16 because it standid ekipment and got more akuracey then a handgun. Goodbye mom. I love you.*

*Jesús your son*

I read the letter with emotion; it was a stirring cry for help. . . . It had come into the right hands too late . . . too late for Jesús, and certainly too late for Agatha Kent.

"Did you discuss the letter with Jesús?"

"Yes. We talked and he told me he couldn't help it, that we were very strict at home, that we had taken him out of the after-school center and away from his friends, that my husband punished him too much when he didn't deserve it, that he was not allowed to go to the movies or do anything he liked, so that he felt like he wanted to kill himself."

"What did your husband do? Did you show him the letter?"

"He never believed that kid talk. He said Jesús wanted me to suffer. I didn't believe that. Jesús was never a mean kid. He was warm. Very warm, and I just don't understand how he changed so soon. My son was complaining to me even before the letter. He said, 'If you don't let me go out, I'm just going to put my head in the TV and I'm going to remember every single TV show there is and maybe someday I'll get to Hollywood. The only things you have left to stop me from doing is breathing and thinking, because I got nothing else to do, just stay home, walk around, watch TV, and sleep.' "

34

"Did you know Mrs. Kent, the lady who lived next door to you?"

"I met the lady, yes, when we moved uptown."

"Did you talk to her?"

"Sometimes we'd say good morning, you know, and hello how are you, that was about it. She was a friendly old lady, maybe a little crazy."

"Did Jesús talk to her?"

"Yes, yes. Once when the three of us were on the front stoop, Jesús, me, and Al, she came to us and told us what a good boy Jesús was, and what a nice family we were."

"Why would she have called Jesús a good boy?"

"Maybe because he used to read the *TV Guide* to her. . . . She lost her glasses one time and he shopped for her too."

As Mrs. Allendez left, she begged me to do what I could to help her boy. I promised I would, and suggested that we meet again to talk, that she had been very helpful.

"I don't know what else I have to tell you," she sighed.

"Don't worry about it," I said, "worry never helps."

# 4

Jesús was late. Not entirely his fault since his escort (a Youth House counselor) was in charge of getting him to me on time. Emergencies at Youth House often required the immediate attention of the entire staff, and so when this happened, things of lesser importance suffered . . . my appointments with Jesús fell into this category. I had already sent in my proposal that he be allowed to receive treatment at my home, as my guest, for a probationary period of time during which I hoped to rehabilitate him. A reply to this sort of proposal was usually slow since it had to go through committee, be reviewed by a board of officials, the facts duplicated on sheet after sheet of mimeograph bond that was then sent around to supplement the agency portfolio. If and when Jesús was released in my custody there would be no wasted time since he would be under my constant benign surveillance.

I reviewed the Allendez File while waiting. There was additional recent material supplied by Nina Allendez: second-grade test material that she had valued and kept as evidence that Jesús had been an intelligent child.

The test was in question/answer form and had been

offered to the entire second grade. I was impressed with the simple, straightforward answers Jesús had given to these elementary queries.

Q: *Why Do We Need To Wear Clothing?* Give as many answers as you can.
A: A child need clothes because its vital parts.
   A child need cloth is to cannot see his body.
   A child need cloding to preserb the warm of the body.

Q: *Why Do We Sleep?* Give as many answers as you can.
A: The dream comes in my head.
   A child sleep because he tired.
   A child sleep to get up in the morning.

Q: *Why Do We Eat?* Give as many answers as you can.
A: When he's hungry.
   For the good taste.
   A child has teeth to chew.
   So he grow big.

When I showed Jesús the test paper (which he had not seen for a long time), he told me that he had been helped with it by a brighter student who had suggested the phrase "vital parts." He also brought up his grandmother, whom he had loved very much. "She teach me things too, and she didn't try to make me wear rubber pants like a baby when I go to sleep. She didn' expect me to train my bladder like it was a dog doing tricks," he said.

"Somebody made you wear rubber pants?"

"That bastard Al . . . I told Mom not to tell him about the wet sheets. I didn' wanna wet them. After a while it gets freezin' . . . and smelly."

The entire office was smelly; I had collected my urine the night before (for this olfactory experiment) and hidden small jars of the watery fluid under the desk, behind the couch, on the bookcase, under the cocktail table, and so forth. Truly, the room contained an odor so memorable one could swear a brigade of bums had marched through. Either Jesús was being polite, or he had not noticed.

"Do you remember when you first started wetting the bed in your sleep?" I asked.

"Maybe when my mom went to New York . . . maybe not . . . maybe before, because she was nervous and crying all the time, and maybe it was because of me. . . . Grandma was mad at Mom before she went away and she was always sayin' about me that I was a poor boy, so I guess I was that poor boy . . . but then Grandma took me everywhere for fun because I was that poor boy."

"Where'd she take you?"

"I saw the place Columbus landed. There's a cross on the beach that mark the spot. I think the place called Doquierre. We was at a crummy hotel; my bed didn' have no mattress. There was a thin quilt over the wire springs. When I got in, you know, I roll to the middle and sink in. The bed was old-fashion and had a canopy made of net and lace, but there was holes in it so the mosquitoes got in anyway. It was sure beautiful. A real artist must of paint it with roses and green leaves on the posts."

"Did you wet that bed?"

"Well, it drip, drip, drip on the floor and I was sorry so I wipe it off the floor with my shirt and hang it on the balcony to dry. . . . Say, no offense, Dr. Brody, but it smell like piss in here. Maybe you should open the window . . . and lissen, I'm sure it ain't me."

"Probably another patient, Jesús. You're not the only one with this problem . . ."

"I glad to hear I ain't one of a kind, Dr. Brody."

"So . . . you were on the balcony?"

"Yeah . . . and when I went on this balcony—thanks for opening the window—when I went on this balcony I watched the funeral of a tiny baby girl. She was small and tiny than I ever saw. Her coffin wasn't no bigger than a cardboard flower box. A man in a pink shirt was carryin' the wood coffin. And it was hot. The sweat pourin' down

38

the man's face. The sun shinin' on the little girl's face. There was a few flowers on her head, like pink and orange. She wore a clean white dress that the flies go on. Grandma tol' me the man carryin' the coffin was a friend of the girl's family and that at the cemetery he was goin' to take her out the box and put her right in the dirt to bury her, and in three years her bones would be dug up and throw them in a pile. So then I got scared and ask Grandma if Mom was dead, and she said, 'No, only your momma's heart is dead.' ''

"Your grandma was using a figure of speech."

"A what?"

"What do you think she meant?"

"About Mom? Well, that her heart stop but her body keep goin' like them chickens without a head that run all over the yard."

"Stop kidding me, Jesús!"

"All right, so Grandma accuse her of havin' a cold heart so far as we was concerned at the time . . . that's it. . . . Right?"

"Do you still think your mother has a cold heart?"

"Maybe it all her fault, the bitch!"

"Your mother's a bitch?"

"Leave it at that, okay?"

"Why?"

" . . . !"

"Answer me!"

"Let's talk about someone who love me . . . Grandma."

"All right."

Jesús and his grandmother had a relationship very much like that between Gorki and his grandmother; Gorki's grandmother protected him from an abusive and violent father and grandfather; she told him stories he would never forget. These grandmothers were the cultural link . . . the enduring love connection.

As Jesús related the past his face took on a happy

39

glow. I marveled at his recall . . . he had been so young
. . . but in his case the past had been the best part.

"When Grandma was eighteen and just married she
lived in the hills of Puerto Rico, I think it was called
Mayaguez, and they had big barrels of water standing
there to use for everything: cooking, washing, to see your
face. . . . Well, she made my grandpa some poached eggs
but that was before she saw that drowned rat in the bar-
rel. She said how she put rat poison all around to kill the
rats, but that it was worse to see all the dead rats laying
around the living room big as cats. Grandma, she make
me avocado salad with them sweet onions. The avocados
with rough skin taste real good. I put lemon on 'em. Well,
far as I know the rats were my only friends . . . I use ta
watch 'em play football, yeah, and do them high hurdles
right in my bedroom. I wasn't scared of 'em, I even touch
one once; it was soft and furry. The disgustin' thing about
rats is their tails. Their sharp teeth ain't so hot neither.
. . . Reminds me of Dracula."

"Dracula?"

"The bloodsucker . . . you know, Dracula has these
sharp fangs that he sinks into his victim's neck. . . . He
could have immoral life if he get enough blood . . . he
never give up. . . . When he drink the blood he stops being
wild, he get like peaceful. That the time to watch out for
Dracula. What you think?"

"I think he's so thin because he's on a liquid diet."

"Doc, you crazy, you know? But really, what you
think?"

"I think Dracula's one hell of a lonely guy."

"Yeah, it's his fate. First people think he's a bad dude,
he come on so suave and all, then the blood craze comes
on him and he offs his friends."

"In other words, Dracula can't help the bad things he
does?"

"No, his life depends on it."

"Therefore he's as doomed as his victims?"

40

"Sounds right."

"What would you do if you were Dracula?"

"If I would be Dracula, I do what Dracula do, or I would be somebody else . . . only all my victims'd be enemies of the U.S.A., that way I have a good rep and be invited to the White House. . . . Dracula already dress formal: white gloves, tails, bow tie, and don't forget his cape. . . . He outclass the President, man!"

A *sociopathic personality* is a psychiatric label that denotes a person who is emotionally cool, feels little in the way of remorse or guilt, has no capacity for empathy, but otherwise presents pretty much the picture of a normal person.

How and why such a person becomes the way he is, is not known, although current theory, inevitably, has to do with inconsistent parenting during early childhood. It has to do with double standards.

The killer one sees on the front pages of tabloids, smiling and cocky, may be the picture of a sociopathic personality. The suspect who leaves a police car and traverses the distance between the police car and the courtroom with a coat over his head may also be a sociopathic personality, one, however, with an eye to the future: if recognized, his life could be in danger. He is not concealing shame, he is reacting to fear of retribution, an anxiety grounded in reality. The pity is that he did not experience this fear before the crime.

I cannot assign blame to parents for not providing appropriate punishment and guidance for a child early in life. There are too many examples of a child growing up mentally healthy in spite of a destructive environment. A person does not deliberately become a sociopath or a useful member of society . . . it just happens.

Moral insanity is another way of saying that the sociopath knows right from wrong, but doesn't care. . . . However, one person's right is another person's wrong. . . . The

41

act itself is not wrong, e.g., shooting a war criminal in the head may be taken in certain situations as virtuous, and the executioner as an exemplary person. Self-defense is another situation in which the killing of a human being exonerates the killer. Who is to say what self-defense is? Is it only the fending off of sudden, physical aggression? The defense of one's own life? What is life-threatening besides actual death? What is living-death? Isn't all life a "life-and-death" situation? When Jesús shot Agatha Kent, was he not defending his own life? Did he have time to know right from wrong when she threatened to call the police? In do-or-die circumstances, the stress of the moment often culminates in someone's death.

Could I substitute the term "Dracula syndrome" for sociopathic personality? May Jesús (Dracula) Allendez then be described as an anguished, eccentric, and somehow charismatic outsider? As a Dracula compulsively driven to commit horrors he himself is curiously detached from?

## ALLENDEZ, JESÚS, FILE

Clipped from the *Regional Enquirer,* a Brooklyn-based tabloid dedicated to the more sensational aspects of local crime, but offering hints on home canning and the latest in cancer cures. Because of its lurid content—describing a latter-day Dracula—I saved it.

### DRIFTER LEAVES BLOODY TRAIL

#### By Ignatius Ditenhaffer

Brooklyn (AP)—When the medical examiner tried to draw blood from the corpses of a Brooklyn Heights couple found dead last September, he couldn't—all the blood had been drained by their murderer.

Police said Thursday the man they are seeking for questioning, a former neighbor of the victims, had a penchant for cutting the heads off rats and draining their blood. Authorities said the man was last seen in Colorado near the scene of where several horses were found dead and drained of blood.

"The man is a drifter who wanders around with his violin and a dog," a member of the homicide squad said, "and he plays Country Western tunes while the dog dances. This is the way he earns a living."

In an unusual show of emotion for an officer of the law, the detective crushed a beer can in one hand as he said, "Can you believe it, this musician used to catch rats in his apartment, cut off their heads, and drain their blood. From what I understand, it was an attention-getter. If someone he felt close to did not appear interested in him any more, he'd do his act and leave the blood on the kitchen table. But don't ask me why."

Another detective suggested that the man had it in for those who had achieved fame playing the fiddle, and was pathologically jealous. . . . Both of his victims had been featured performers on "Grand Ole Opry" before moving East.

# 5

Allison Kent had guessed that the way to my heart was through my filing cabinet where, arranged alphabetically, according to client, crisp oak-tag folders held all sorts of information. Her still slender dossier carried, like a tiny ship on the horizon, her name typed on a raised piece of paper enclosed protectively within a quarter-inch rectangle of stiff red cellophane. I kept a box of these pretty name carriers in my desk drawer with other office supplies. Dipping at random into my cache, I had taken the color yellow for Jesús. The color had no significance and was just as transparent as the rest. At a glance, and by color, I could select the file I wanted. Sometimes I would just slide my fingers across these name tags, bending them a little . . . thinking.

"This is Mom's obituary," she said. "I clipped it from the *New York Times.* Funny how they keep the information in their morgue, and then when someone dies *it* comes to life!"

"I see that your mother was somewhat of a celebrity in her youth," I observed while reading the obit.

"She was a lesser Isadora Duncan," Allison said proudly.

## KENT, ALLISON, FILE

### AGATHA KENT DANCE INNOVATOR

*Charmed Heads of State at Six Years of Age*

Agatha Kent, one of America's least-known pioneers in the modern dance, died June 3, a victim of the crime of murder, at her home in Washington Heights. She was eighty-three years old.

Although Mrs. Kent originated the "free and easy" mode of dance technique in which the dancer wears opaque veils tied about her waist which others in the company hold onto as they whirl about, credit was unfairly given to Isadora Duncan, who also went barefoot and embraced the naked pillars of ancient temples. However, Mrs. Kent did not let public opinion, or credit withheld, stand in her way. The late Mischa Goss, news editor of *Dancer From the Dance* magazine, once said of her as a performer: "Agatha Kent came up with a startling innovation called 'Dancing the Truth.' Each concert was a diary of what she had done that very day. Her work, both spontaneous and at times withdrawn (she often sat on stage with her back to the audience till she pronounced herself ready), had a freshness that only someone's real story can have. She did not have to search for material; her own life lent itself to her art." Speaking of Mrs. Kent's activities on behalf of modern dance, her daughter, Allison Kent, observed: "When my mother entered the field, she appeared to be some wild-eyed eccentric out to shock the middle class; she did more than that, she was a genius of the American theater."

45

## Parents Were Union Officials

The daughter of Clarence and Winnie Laub, both members of the National Confederation of Hatters and Milliners, Mrs. Kent was born in Oberlin, Ohio, on June 4, 1896.

At the age of six she was taken to Vienna, where her parents considered the purchase of a hat factory. While there she was persuaded to dance for a bald gentleman who had been discussing terms of the sale with her father. She took a few steps, both mincing and gliding in the manner of an agile six-year-old, then removed her panties and fitted them over a hand-carved wooden hat block that sat *sans cloche* on a shelf. The bald gentleman, who had seen many a dance in his day, told her parents that she would go far.

At the age of fourteen she was awarded a small portable stage made of resilient wood, which she installed in Central Park just beyond the Metropolitan Museum of Art, and gave concerts there. Mrs. Kent soon became involved with New York cultural life, and her friends included Carl Sandburger, Henry Mueller, Edna St. Barnabas Frisée, Dalia Croze, Igor Strumsky, and José Lemur.

At sixteen, deciding she wanted to be a choreographer, she formed her own company. "I'm really a tough character," she said. "I can make a dancer out of anyone, and they don't need both legs either!" Eventually she choreographed the *Squatting and Rising Chain,* using only one-legged dancers. This triumph did not hold her for long.

In 1918 she was married to Karl Kent, who operated a popular Manhattan restaurant, French and Fries, whose menu offered both a French and Anglo-Saxon cuisine. When she was no longer able to dance at her desired weight, they were divorced.

## Invited

She worked on technique alone for a year and then reappeared as a featured dance attraction at the Down Pillow Performing Arts Festival. She also occasionally wrote essays on the dance for magazines and souvenir programs under the pseudonym Julia Sorel. These essays extolled American dance as diary and urged Americans to shed their cultural inferiority complex. She was equally unsuccessful in getting them to shed their cultural housing complexes: "People are unwilling to abandon their real estate for a season ticket to the dance theater," she declared.

## Active in Brooklyn

Mrs. Kent was also active in the Brooklyn Society, and in 1960 helped found its Outpost Arts Program.

She received the *Dance* magazine award in 1963, at a time when she had turned to volunteer work in veterans hospitals, for "humanistic reasons." "Better late than never," she commented. In 1973 she was honored at a gala reception at the Kennedy Center for the Performing Arts. A movie of her life composed of footage from dance archives was hastily edited and presented before a distinguished audience which included the President and his immediate family.

## Survived by

She is survived by a daughter, Allison Kent, who resides in Canada. A son, Karl Kent, Jr., died in 1958. Mrs. Kent's former husband, Karl Kent, died in 1948.

Nurses struck Presbyterian, Kingsbrook, Jewish, and Maimonides hospitals a week ago before reaching agreements on new contracts. The funeral will be private. A memorial service will be announced at a later date, said yesterday that Long Island and New

York City retailers had experienced a "drop-off" in usage of about 11.5 percent.

"The last paragraph is a typographical error," Allison explained, "but they refused to print a correction under errata. How insensitive!"

"Yes, you must be very upset."

"I've filed suit."

"Better to take action than to stew. There's a theory, similar to the one on psychosomatic illness, that people who stew tend to boil out the valuable vitamins and minerals that make them healthy."

"There's more. . . . Something even worse happened at Momma's funeral . . . I almost had a heart attack. . . . Momma's body broke through the bottom of the casket as it was being carried to her grave; they had surrounded her body with rags, newspapers, shredded paper, and rolled-up panty hose. . . . Don't you think they might have used more respectful materials to cushion Momma with? Even foam rubber or excelsior would have done the trick."

I nodded in agreement. It was a scene fit for a horror movie. Allison continued. "I'm filing a damage suit against the casket firm and the funeral parlor, charging misuse of funds and misrepresentation. . . . Do you think you could testify on my behalf?" She leaned forward, waiting for my answer, one hand nervously plucking her jacket sleeve.

"I wasn't there, Allison."

"I mean would you be willing to send a letter saying that the shock caused me emotional and physical distress . . ."

"I might be . . ."

". . . and the loss of life's enjoyment? I'm nervous, I shake, I can't sleep, and I have nightmares. It's true."

"How much are you asking?"

"In excess of one million."

"Do you think the money would cure you of these symptoms?"

"Definitely, Dr. Brody. I couldn't be unhappier than I am now."

"Do you feel that in some way you're responsible for what happened?"

"NO! Well, perhaps I should have been there to supervise. . . . I took care of the arrangements by phone . . . just wanted to get it over with."

"You wouldn't have been allowed in the mortuary, Allison. . . . I'm sure you're not the first customer they've taken advantage of."

"Maybe not. They get you when you're most vulnerable and profit from it. Are you sure I couldn't have done something about it? What if I had been rich and appeared at the funeral home dressed in mink and diamonds? Would they have dared to do what they did?"

"Probably would have taken you for more," I said. "Get off your guilt trip, Allison."

"Guilt trip?"

"Guilt is a trip, you know; one starts out with poor accommodations so as to be uncomfortable along the way . . . the destination, ostensibly, is a place where one can relax and cast off worries and recriminations. . . . However, it is possible to reach the same destination if one travels deluxe. In the long run, first class is cheaper. Change your reservations, Allison; enjoy life."

"I'll try, Doctor."

"Now, let's choose another time to meet."

". . . I just remembered something I want to tell you . . . do we have time?"

"What is it?"

"I've never been lonelier in my life."

"We'll talk about it next time, Allison. Try not to forget what you wanted to discuss. Write it down if you have to, but remember, loneliness is only the tip of the iceberg; it's going to take a long time to melt whatever's below the waterline; but while we're waiting for the thaw, try to appreciate the penguins, the sunrise, and the sunset . . . wave to the ships that pass in the night."

## KENT, ALLISON, FILE

*To Whom It May Concern,*

*My client Allison Kent, who is presently in consultation with me, has suffered severe psychological damage as the result of a recent occurrence involving the memorial service and interment of her mother, Mrs. Agatha Kent. As the casket in which Mrs. Kent's body lay was being carried to her grave, the bottom of the box, made of shoddy materials, gave way, and Mrs. Kent's body, accompanied by a shower of shredded paper, rags, and other packing materials, fell through. The sight of her mother exposed to all, on the grass—a grotesque sight to be sure—caused Allison Kent immediate and grievous shock, the results of which continue to this day: she has nightmares, cannot hold a job, her hair has turned white overnight, and a benign cystic condition of the breasts threatens to become malignant. This is my considered professional opinion. Should it become necessary, I am willing to present my viewpoint in the courtroom.*

*Sincerely,*

*Mathilda Brody*

*Mathilda Brody, Ph.D., M.D., F.A.A.P.*

# 6

---

I had been waiting for word from the Project Committee on whether or not my proposal to have Jesus "stay close" to me in a natural environment, my home, had been approved. There was disagreement among them as to exactly what benefit this would be to the patient since he had already made an adjustment to prison life and had been singled out by the civilian librarian to assist him. Furthermore, Dr. I. C. Dacks had applied for additional funding to continue his project: the testicular measurement of boys admitted to the center to determine if there was any correlation between a youth's sexual development and his propensity for crime. Dr. Dacks had been collecting his data for four years and required at least one more in order to analyze the information. A similar project conducted at the Women's House of Detention had brought much interpenal fame to the investigating team there, along with additional funding and a medical "free hand" to use the money as they saw fit. This concentration on genitalia (a minor obsessive trait, rampant within the profession) could, as far as I could see, serve no useful

51

purpose; however, my opinion had not been asked for, and any interjection by me would have been misconstrued (thought to be prompted wholly by self-interest).

By chance, a forgotten pocket of money was found; it had been targeted for the purchase of uniforms and new equipment in the medical sector, but since the time period during which these improvements were to be made had passed, and the accounting department wanted to balance its books before the end of the year, the vagrant funds were conveniently allocated to me. How long this funding would last I could only guess. Whether or not the committee would grant me an extension when I needed it would depend entirely on their interpretation of a quarterly report concerning my project. On such a slender thread does the advancement of science often hang.

I explained to Harry that I was about to have Jesús as a houseguest.

"You'll have to stay away for a while."

"I don't see why. I'm gone most of the day. I won't interfere."

"I'd feel your presence, even if I didn't see you. I must be alone with my work."

"Alone with your work?"

"Yes. It's important to create an incubation environment for the little chick. I'm giving Jesús a second chance. Actually, a first chance."

"Playing God, or just playing?"

"Both."

"Where does that leave me?"

"You have your involvements, I have mine."

"Isn't it dangerous being alone with such a person?"

"Raissa is here. Besides, I think by now I'm able to judge the mental states of my patients. . . . Jesús has had his episode of violence, it won't happen again."

"Madame Curie thought she knew the properties of radium . . ."

"For God's sake, Harry! Why are you trying to undermine my efforts!"

"You're the doctor, you tell me."

"You're jealous."

"My dear, you're asking me to stay away. . . . This is my home away from home."

"We're not joined at the hip, Harry, the separation won't kill you."

"That's a very hostile remark, Mathilda. Shall I leave now?"

"I apologize . . . I do intend to keep in touch. I need you."

"For what?"

"For you. You always help to clarify my thoughts. You're the man in the street."

"Now what the hell does that mean?"

"I think like a scientist, and you think like an ordinary person . . . an intelligent ordinary person."

"You know I love you, but I can't promise complete fidelity when we're apart."

"I don't expect it. At any rate, our lovemaking is secondary to other things in our relationship. . . . It's become damned obligatory, Harry . . . something I could do without."

"You don't enjoy me in bed? Since when?"

"Since I have other things on my mind. I wouldn't enjoy anyone."

"Oh . . . things on your mind. Look, I've got things on my mind too."

I helped Harry get his things together and put them in an overnight bag.

"I'll call you, darling," he said. "Maybe you'll miss me."

"Yes, do . . . dinner is always a possibility. . . . And, Harry, of course I'll miss you."

The first night Jesús stayed with me he had a vision. It might have been anticipated because of his anxiety related to the move; in effect, he was under house arrest, no freer than he had been in the youth facility, even though all the comforts of home were now available to him.

He asked me, "What good is me stayin' here? I can't get no parole for twenty-five years anyway. When they let me go I'll be an old man. I'll be 'bout forty years old!"

"Whether or not you benefit from your stay here is up to you, Jesús . . . besides, forty isn't so old; I'm nearly forty myself."

"What if I try to escape? Ain't you takin' a chance keepin' me here?"

"Yes, I'm taking a chance . . . but if you try to escape you'll be losing all this."

"Doc, you don't understand. I ain't got nothin' to lose!"

"I'm sorry you feel like that," I said, "but it won't always be that way. You'll have plenty to lose before we're through."

His room was neat and impersonal; it met his obsessional standards: bed tightly made, bare floor, one modern floor lamp, a table/desk, Sony clock/radio, pillow rolled into a lozenge shape and jammed against the wall, stubby enameled chest of drawers. What he brought with him barely filled one drawer: socks, jocks, jeans, shirts, and a hairbrush. Jesús had not heard the advice usually given a homesick traveler. "Carry something with you that reminds you of home: a picture you can hang in some far-off hotel room, your own colorful bedspread, a pair of favorite candlesticks for late dinner in your room, incense to give a hint of exotica, a photo-album to place on your

54

night table." If Jesús was a tourist, his present itinerary was (of necessity) unfortunately limited, and gave him no pleasure.

"How did you sleep?" I asked him.

He shrugged his shoulders. "Didn't."

"Not at all?"

"I don't think so . . . about eleven or eleven-thirty the moon came on the wall opposite me. It was dark in the room except for that."

"Can you describe it more precisely?"

"It was round, about as big as the top of a coffee can, and it move slowly across the room, getting higher and higher."

"What would you say it was made of?"

"Nothing . . . just light . . . you could almost see through it."

"Was it the same as, let us say, the light in the hall-way?"

"No, because the light didn't stay in the circle, it went out of the edges and was shaky."

"As if it wanted to escape?"

"It just wanted to fill the room I think. I couldn't get my eyes off it . . . thought that if I looked away somethin' terrible would happen. I had to be real careful."

"Didn't you wonder a bit when you suddenly saw this thing? Did you think I'd hung a Japanese lantern in your room?"

"No, Doc, I knew right away what it meant. I wanted to go up and touch it, but I only touch it with my eyes. I was afraid and stayed in bed."

"Just why did you use the word moon to refer to this phenomenon?"

"All day I was thinking about the moon: how pale, how cold, and how it was like a big blind eye that didn't want to see what was down in the world . . . didn't want

55

to see Brunetti dead. . . . It hurt me when Brunetti left me
. . . and I had the feeling that he went up to the moon
. . . so, I was afraid that if I stopped looking at the moon
on the wall, the real moon would come close to earth and
I'd have to get on it to be with Brunetti again . . . and dead
like him."

For a person with so many problems, Jesús certainly
had had many friends . . . this is of course possible with the
sociopath who is adept at hiding his true self (a favorite
trick also of the psychotic and the borderline schizoid
personality). This is also true of most analysts (but for
different reasons and with divergent but not dissimilar
results).

"Who is Brunetti?" I asked Jesús. "You haven't mentioned him before." Brunetti could have been an imaginary friend, or the name Jesús had given to another part
of himself (sometimes when a split occurs, the personality
divides into two: the good self and the bad self . . . the bad
self wants to die . . . the good self wants to live; but if the
good self is imaginary it is already dead).

"Wasn't important before," he answered.

"But now it is?"

"Didn't want it to be . . . wanted to forget him. Brunetti was a great guy. We did everything together until he
drowned two years ago. . . . His mother act mad to me.
Even my mom was lookin' at me as if it was my fault. Well,
I thought, 'How come?' Like I was alive and he was dead.
In school they give him a special auditorium with two
minutes of silence to remember him by. Hey, I remember
him without the two minutes. We used to dive off that
rock up the Hudson where the ferry go by. When he
drown, the people on the ferry was still handin' cans of
beer to the other guys who was swimmin' over. We used
to dive for the beer. It was kicks."

"You can't bring the good times back . . . but the bad
times won't go away, will they, Jesús?" I said sympatheti-
cally.

"No, Doc."

"And you did resist stepping on the moon and leaving us forever, didn't you?"

"That right, Doc."

I continued, trying to make his episode of depersonalization a positive occurrence. "You toughed it out, frightening as it was; you did the right thing. I'm proud of you, Jesús . . . I really am." In his entire lifetime no one had ever said that to him. Someone more sophisticated would have thought I was mocking him, but Jesús was in such great need that he accepted the compliment. What I had meant was that I was glad he was alive.

In analysis, the doctor must wait till the patient is ready before destroying his defenses. This Hans Christian Andersen story illustrates my point: A little girl has a ribbon tied around her neck. She is asked to remove it. The person making the request does not ask herself, "Is the ribbon a decoration or does it have some utility?" She cannot see beyond the ribbon. As a consequence, when the ribbon is untied the little girl's head falls off. (The ribbon concealed a deep wound that had not yet healed.) Slowly . . . slowly was the way to go with Jesús.

For one whole day Jesús would not get out of bed. I refused to serve him his food there.

"What's the matter?" I asked him.

"Nothin'."

"Aren't you hungry?"

"No."

"Aren't you getting enough attention?"

"Yeah."

"Then get out of bed."

"No."

"Won't you tell me what's wrong?"

"Can't say it to you."

"Why?"

"It too private."

"I'm in the private business, tell me."

"All right . . . you ask for it. Well, I'm afraid . . . that something . . . will go up my ass."

"What?"

"Something . . . it give me a headache . . . maybe my troubles is some feelings I don't understand."

"Does it have to do with yesterday's talk? With your friend Brunetti?"

"Maybe . . . like when he ask me if I ever thought about doin' it with a guy . . . I'm not sure if he meant with him. Sometimes he do anything."

"Why do you think he asked you?"

"Maybe he could see something."

"See what?"

"Maybe he thought I was a fag."

"Is that what you're worried about?"

"No, because if anyone ever tried that, to make me a girl, I'd kill 'em or be killed myself."

Shame. Guilt. And lying. The first week Jesús had been at the facility he had been sodomized. He had not retaliated. The examining doctor, Dr. Menninger Hong-Harvey, a proctologist who had received his training in Haiti and was highly proficient in the use of herbs, salves, and potions, had noted a violently ripped sphincter resulting from numerous, consecutive, forced entries: he had ordered Jesús into the hospital to heal.

Any justice is poetic to those who demand it. It is the only poetry written into law or regularly recited by the defenseless. Judging from the following description of castration meted out to a rapist (originally published in *Our Neighbors in the Mid-East: A Monthly Journal for Scholars*), such poetry is not confined to the West.

. . . the castrating instrument, similar in appearance to an aluminum snail tongs, having a powerful and taut spring with which it is hinged . . . man tied to an unfinished board

58

... flap cut in his pants above his genitals ... has been given something to drink ... alcohol subdues him ... is quiet, but fear not totally insulated . . . the occasional shiver . . . scrotum soft as curdled milk draw themselves up . . . like eyes rolling in their sockets the testes tense inwards ... ties off this double pouch with strong, narrow cord . . . he begins the process toward isolation and loss . . . ligature stops the bleeding and nothing else . . . crushing force of the castrating instrument ... first ... cord is pulled tighter . . . it is not enough to release the "balls" from where they are rooted . . . razor is swiftly drawn across the base . . . wobbly mass drops into sawdust . . . no involuntary erection here as in death . . . no final spitting of semen . . . dribble of urine watery and pale . . . a scream emerges at a distance from its origin . . . the ventriloquist's art in the rapist's mouth ... he will not die but will continue to suffer . . . healing powders are applied to the wound . . .

Sodomy may serve the same purpose (as castration) in a delicately balanced male; however, one is reversible, the other is not. Jesús was raped, yes, but it did not help him to identify with his own rape victim Agatha Kent (who had been forced by him into a condition of irreversibility). Death, unfortunately, is not a raincoat that can be worn inside out. One might say that such a raincoat has a double life, and is an economical purchase. . . . Death has its own economy; it needs nothing.

Harry says that homosexual violence is no worse than any other kind of violence; he speaks of "fist-fucking," the first choice of elite sodomites who want to be entered in a way that is physically extreme.

"It has to do with relaxation," Harry explained. "I've seen objects bigger than a fist enter the anus. Sometimes there is injury . . . a tear similar to the perineal tear during a difficult childbirth. Yes, it is painful even with lubrication . . . I attest to that, however, the pleasure is more intense . . . and one is being used in the most intimate sense . . . one cannot protect oneself from the onslaught."

"But using egress for ingress, Harry, isn't that laying waste; pardon the pun."

Harry looked at me with his large, brown, doleful eyes. "Mathilda, this is serious stuff we're talking about. It has to do with being dominated, with being of service, with complete confidence . . ."

"With the changing of diapers, Harry. With the display of one's bottom for Mommy to wipe . . . only you're speaking of a mean mommy who must be shown she is doing harm. As the masochistic receptor, it is you who have the upper hand . . . you who are leading the parade backward."

"No, no, Mathilda . . . it is not about the past . . . it is about the desired effect."

"Which is what, Harry?"

"Erection and orgasm."

"Is that all there is, my friend?"

"Sometimes there's dinner afterward."

A masochist is a masochist no matter the method he (or she) chooses to exercise punishment upon himself. It is like a game of hot potato: one person gets burned and hurriedly passes the pain onto the next in line. I am thinking here of my own relationship with Harry. Why would I have chosen a man whose primary desire is for men? Where is my self-esteem? And why is Harry constantly scratching his pubic area? Can it be body lice?

The doctor did find a tiny egg glued to Harry's pubic region, when he examined it with a battery-lit magnifying glass. He recommended that Harry drench the area, for two nights, with a preparation called Kwell.

"How did you become infected?" I asked Harry.

"Must have been the steam room, I didn't sit on a towel," he answered.

"Sure you didn't inherit your crabs during a sexual encounter?"

"Certainly not!" he replied.

Rear entry gives me no pleasure, but since Harry's

fantasies are about men, I allow it. My generosity enables him to be potent with me. It is an activity of the most intimate nature. A male receiving the penis within his rectum receives pleasure this way because the glands that have to do with erection are massaged by such an entry.

Mother and vagina are synonymous in some men's minds . . . mother is a virgin in perpetuity, particularly postpartum, no matter how many times she splits open to deliver a child to the world. Having arrived safely, but not without trauma, the male often fears a repeat entrapment within this adaptable foyer, and invests it with powers it does not have: e.g., the power to remove the penis with something as efficient as a LawnBoy mower, or the teeth of a piranha. The male overvalues his organ. He thinks everyone wants it. He thinks that if he is not careful he will lose it. As proof, he indicates with chagrin the daily tumescence and detumescence of the penis. Ideally, he would have it remain erect (inconveniently), a prefab monument to itself, not dependent on erotic signals that may or may not work. This erotic signal is never the mother, and preferably not anyone remotely resembling her. Thus the classic division of woman into two kinds of women: the virgin and the whore. This division was perpetrated in fear, and sustained in fear by the male who dares not trespass lest he be emasculated. A male who is adept at erecting pedestals will not have much luck in erecting penises.

"The rectum is a mock vagina," I said to Harry. "Who's kidding who?"

*"Inter urinas et faeces nascimur,"* he answered cleverly, quoting St. Augustine. " 'We are born among feces and urine.' "

What that had to do with his preference for sodomy, I could not guess, but the statement did indicate that our natures are opposed to our civilized norms.

# 7

I took Raissa to Dr. Kohlmar for a checkup. She seemed to be suffering a personality change: slept a lot, did not eat well.

"She's getting old," he said. "Teeth are a trouble source. When animals can't chew, the jig's up." He cleaned her teeth.

"What about this lump under her flesh here on the neck," I asked.

"Fatty tissue or a benign tumor; not to worry, she's in good shape for an old lady," he reassured me.

"What the doctor say about Raissa?" Jesús asked.

"She's okay," I answered.

"Well, that the best news, ain't it!" he said. "Once I had a dog same as you. Grandma got him for me. He was cute. I gotta admit it. Just a puppy. He sleep with me and lick my face. Well, then there was fleas in the bed too. Grandma didn't like for him to get in the bed. She yell at him and he run away. I loved her, but *que mujer brava!*"

"What does that mean?"

"Means, 'What a vicious woman!' " Jesús explained.

"You hated her for chasing the puppy out of your bed?"

"I was just mad. And then it really got worse. Everybody was talkin' about the bubonic plague; how it was going around . . . so all the dogs had to be killed. It was shitty. Grandma bury Doggy in the garden and put a white cross over his grave, then she wrote 'To the memory of Doggy who never hurt anyone and who everyone love' on a piece of wood and nailed it to the cross. Shows Grandma really love Doggy. That surprise me all right. For a few night I stay on his grave. They had to pull me off."

"You blame your grandmother?"

"She could've hid him. He wasn't sick."

"But it's the fleas that spread the plague and you did say that Doggy had fleas."

"Yeah? So what!"

"If Doggy had been spared, perhaps others would have died in consequence, including you and your grandmother."

"Who cares, who cares, who cares!" he shouted. Before he could throw the paperweight from my desk across the room, Raissa rushed up and leaned on him, growling. The paperweight dropped to the floor.

"Down, Raissa! Down!" I ordered.

The dog, satisfied that I was not going to be attacked, returned to her warm place on the rug.

I put my arms around Jesús. "I care," I said, holding him tightly, "that's why I have you here. I care about you."

He tried to squirm out of the hold, but I would not let go until he had calmed down.

"The wrong people in the wrong places always care about me," he said.

"And I am one of those wrong people?" I asked.

63

"You're not my family," Jesús answered, "and this ain't my home."

"It's all the home you've got right now, and lucky to have it too. We do argue like a family, don't we?" I smiled and gave him a hug. "Come off it, Allendez, I have my limits too."

"Yeah? You ever get angry enough to . . ."

"Kill?"

"Yeah."

"Yes."

"But you ain't never done it."

"No . . . but I've come close. Many people have."

"I thought not so many. Say, how close did you come?"

"Right up to the line, but something stopped me."

"What?"

"I don't know . . . something inside."

"Something inside didn't stop me. That's the trouble."

Agatha Kent's murder was caused in part by the Allendez boy's contempt for our society which he perceived as chaotic, malevolent, and repressive: the heart of any definition of evil. Though his act was evil (resulting in the total repression of a life), he was not an evil person. He was a victim (Dracula). As I said to Jesús, "Dracula's one hell of a lonely guy."

## ALLENDEZ, JESÚS, FILE

NOTE: In order to exist at all, Dracula has to drain the blood of other living creatures, after which they in turn become vampires. (Does this involuntary conscription to swell the ranks of the vampires make them any less lonely?)

Does Dracula remember the taste of birth blood? The taste of blood comes before the taste of milk. True oral-regression returns to the taste of blood . . . a time of passivity . . . of latency (it is the beginning).

As long as Dracula can suck on women he does not have to suck on men: the neck's symbolism is obvious. Therefore, the women Dracula loves/attacks are phallic women. . . . Is it safe to say, then, that Jesús has a taste for blood?

With a portion of the funding I had received, I bought a video setup to tape some of our sessions. Therapy would be showtime; instant-replay a bulwark against the tricks that memory plays. A week after our "Doggy" session, the equipment was delivered.

"I'm here." Jesús startled me. I looked up from my notes.

"What were you doing? You're late."

"Combing my hair. Gotta get it right."

"You look fine; you'll see. The equipment's all set up."

Jesus examined the camera, the TV, the room. "What I'm supposed to do now?" he asked.

"What we talked about last night . . . do a TV show like "Kojak." You pick who you want to be, and I'll play someone else, maybe, because I've got to handle the camera. . . . You're the star."

"Know what?" Jesus said. "Mrs. Kent got the same name as Clark Kent."

I think this was the first, no, the second (?) time Jesús had mentioned his victim's name voluntarily.

"Are you speaking of Clark Kent, the mild-mannered reporter of the *Daily Planet*, who becomes Superman?" I asked, wondering what this had to do with the TV drama we were about to improvise.

"You think that old lady was his mother, or his sister or something?"

"Why do you ask?"

"You know why."

"No, I honestly don't."

"You do know! You know that if she's his mom, then he find me here one a these days and kill me!"

"Superman?"

"Sure!"

"I think the name is mere coincidence. Superman would never have allowed you to go as far as you did if his mother had been in danger. He would have rescued her."

"Yeah, I think you're right, Dr. Brody . . . but something's screwy."

"What?"

"*Somebody* wrote about me and Mrs. Kent in the paper. *Somebody* said that the city isn't safe no more. Then the Mayor's office promised action and they caught me. Who do you think got the scoop? Clark Kent!"

"Neither Clark Kent nor Superman exist."

"Yes, he do."

"You exist and I exist."

"Seen Superman in the movies. He real, all right; kissing Lois Lane, destroying the forces of evil, getting to his job on time."

"That was an actor playing Superman."

"So you say . . . but I know he's after my ass 'cause of Mrs. Kent."

"Look, does Superman have a sister?"

"No."

"Well, Mrs. Kent had a daughter. It's a different Kent family. . . . I can show you the newspaper accounts. No one's after you."

"Let's drop it, Dr. Brody. I know different."

There are at least two ways to gain notoriety if one is not a celebrity oneself: one, is *to kill* a celebrity; two, is *to be killed by* a celebrity. Since it is impossible to destroy Superman (many have tried, all have failed), Jesús chose to be destroyed by Superman. To be worthy of such a death, one would have had to commit a crime equal to

66

the hoped-for punishment. By raping and murdering (in his mind), Clark Kent's mother, Jesús had made himself a qualified candidate for status-extinction. Perhaps this analysis is too easy . . . there are other things at work: certainly Superman could be the physical manifestation of Jesús's superego (Superman as super good guy) who knows that the sin committed was wishful matricide, and since Superman is the other side of the Jesús coin (good guy), it would be Jesús (bad guy) killing his own mother, and Jesús (good guy) punishing himself. It was indeed unfortunate that Agatha Kent carried a surname so pregnant with associations for Jesús Allendez.

Though his entire construct was mildly schizophrenic, his pain was not so great that there was danger of dementia. Jesús would not become a vegetable. More likely, if breakdown occurred again he'd be a machine; a television whose box/body already contained the past, the present, and the future, just as the human body does. The television is a happiness machine where, presumably, if one watches long enough, one will be able to see pictures of the primal scene.

Is that what Jesús was waiting for? A "Midnight Blue" presentation featuring his mother as porno-queen (box within a box)? How old had he been when she first performed the Two-Headed Monster for him (her tiny voyeur, eye pressed to a crack in the door). And was he there when the show resumed with a new participant, his stepfather Al, in New York?

"When you feel lonely you can call your mother," I said. "She'd like to hear from you even though she can't visit yet."

"Sure, sure!" Jesús responded. "But I can't stand it when she cries."

It is well known that the primal-scene is enough to traumatize a child. . . . Though children love being frightened (it is then permissible for them to scream and clutch at each other, to experience sexual tension) they do not enjoy thoughts that Daddy is killing Mommy (never the reverse, surprisingly enough). Punch and Judy are potentially dangerous to the psyches of children (though they go at it *fully clothed*); observe these children as they join in a frenzy of mass hysteria while watching angry domestic puppets beat each other silly. They are being titillated by violence! They are laughing at the infliction of pain! If, perhaps, a child could see Mommy and Daddy making love, instead of wondering what goes on behind closed doors (what horrors elicit such groans and cries) trauma might be avoided.

Imagine the Beast with Two Heads, its body rising and falling magically, grunting, sighing, mumbling, shrieking! What fun for a child to see and hear. Is Daddy hurting Mommy? No . . . Mommy and Daddy are putting on a show.

If Jesús had been present during such an act, he most certainly would have been entertained by it and not terrified, although, when one thinks again about his bedwetting, one is led to believe that this renal incontinence is really a letting go of intense sexual tension in response to such stimulation. . . . Putting out the fire, as Freud said, more or less.


"So, let's try the TV thing," I suggested. "Get over there behind the desk."

"Behind the desk?"

"Pretend it's a pile of crates you're hiding behind."

"Hiding from who?"

"Kojak."

"He's a good guy. . . . Let me be Kojak. . . ."

"You want to be a good guy?"

"Sometimes I'm a good guy, and sometimes I'm a bad guy. On the TV it upset me when the cop get killed. If a crook get killed I be upset too. Most times it make me sick if the bad guy get it! That the way I am."

"How'd you feel when you got caught?"

"Like shit. Whatdya think?"

"I think it's second nature for you to be the bad guy."

"Second nature? What's my first nature?"

"To be a good guy. That's everybody's first nature."

"Is there a third nature?"

"That's what you're forming now; your third nature."

"Is it good or bad?"

"An amalgam."

"What the hell's that?"

"A working combination . . . a little of this and a little of that."

"Yeah, but I still want to be Kojak. I can be him *and* the crook. I can change my voice. Wanna hear?"

"It's your show, try it."

I retreated behind the camera. Jesús dodged behind the desk.


## ALLENDEZ, JESÚS, FILE

### TV DETECTIVE DRAMA

### INT. WAREHOUSE DAY

JESÚS hiding behind a pile of crates has been traced to his hideaway by KOJAK. KOJAK believes that JESÚS has raped and killed his niece SOPHIE.

SOUND: *A dog snoring in the locked warehouse office.*

JESÚS
Don't come no closer. I got you covered.

JESÚS rushes out. He drops to the floor, his gun aimed at the desk. He is now KOJAK.

69

KOJAK
Give up, punk, or I'll blow your head off. Why
you wanna live anyway?

KOJAK hears a noise. He shoots his gun in the direction of the
noise. JESÚS runs behind the desk.

JESÚS
That wasn't me, Kojak. That was rats. They
gonna bite your bones now.

JESÚS skids across the floor to lie on his belly. He becomes
KOJAK.

KOJAK
Yeah?! I got a feelin' it gonna be your bones the
rat gonna chew, baby. Don't make a move, mo-
thah.

KOJAK rushes behind the desk. He becomes JESÚS.

JESÚS
Why you after me? I ain't done nothin'.

JESÚS drops to the floor in front of the desk. He becomes
KOJAK.

KOJAK
Drop the gun, sucker, or the gun gonna drop
you. You know why I'm after your ass, baby
... you bastard ... you asshole ... you scumbag,
prick-face, low-life jerk! You raped my lovely
niece Sophie and threw her in the water to die
in the middle of sharks and shit. Remember
Sophie?

KOJAK sneaks closer to the desk. He runs behind it and is once
again the criminal JESÚS.

#### JESÚS
Yeah, Kojak, I recall that whore. She wasn't much. She take my money and rat to the cops, then she take it on the lam and hide out in a posh condominium out Miami Beach way. The lady give me VD.

There is a struggle behind the desk. KOJAK subdues JESÚS. KOJAK retrieves JESÚS's gun from the floor.

#### KOJAK
I'm doin' you a favor to let you live, baby. . . . And if you confess I got a chocolate tootsie-pop for you. You like tootsie-pops?

#### JESÚS
They ain't bad.

#### KOJAK
I'm takin' you in, Jesús . . . and by the time we get to the station house, you better love tootsie-pops better than you momma . . . you better beg me for a tootsie-pop on your knees.

#### JESÚS
You know what you can do with your tootsie-pops!

#### KOJAK
You're screwin' with the wrong cookie, shit-head, 'cause I'm gonna see to it personally that you're sent up for the limit.

JESÚS makes a run for it. He knocks chairs down. Books fall off the table. RAISSA trots after him barking. JESÚS stumbles and falls, mortally wounded by a bullet from KOJAK's gun. His legs thrash about. He groans. Then he lies still. . . . He is dead.

"Boy, it really good to be Kojak," Jesús said, "to be on the side of justice and truth, and to catch worms like me . . . that the greatest. After all . . . I deserve all I get. . . . Except one thing; that Sophie really was a bitch!"

"You mean Sophie's a real person?"

"She that hooker, laid me in the motel."

There are reasons for everything, and every little reason has a reason all its own. In what way, I wondered, did the "Kojak" series resemble primal-scene events? I toyed with the idea that Kojak (the bald man) was Jesús's superego, holding dangerous impulses at a distance. Then I toyed with the idea that the bald head itself was the male genital. Therefore, what I had by accepting this idea was a living "prick" who dispensed minipricks in the shape of tootsie-pops for others and himself to suck on (a covert homosexual activity).

But what about the women in these episodes? With no women it is almost impossible to have a primal-scene. Sometime ago I did view an episode involving a prostitute, but she had to be sacrificed (shot down in cold blood) by show's end. This dubious morality of having certain classes of people more dispensable than others had always bothered me. Do only "good" people deserve to live? Those singled out for a "who cares anyway" elimination are society's outcasts, those who are already punished by their lack of status: the poor, the sick, the sexually promiscuous, the mentally impaired, etc. I found myself ready to abandon my theory that the television set is a happiness machine, where, if one watches long enough, one will be able to see pictures of the primal-scene. A substitute theory: the television set is a retribution machine, where, if one watches long enough, one dies a thousand deaths.

"I was on the roof before," Jesús said in a strained voice.

72

"Why the roof? I don't allow you on the roof." Had he contemplated suicide? Had I missed a clue even while mulling over the complicated material he had presented in the last week?

"I was waiting for Superman, to see if he would come and get me. I gave him his chance. Now I'm sure. He ain't after me. So I went to sleep."

"I'm glad nobody's after you," I said.

"He's still my friend. Just like he's Jimmy's friend."

"Jimmy?"

"Yeah, the kid who work at the *Daily Planet.* I like to work on a newspaper, but my chance is past."

"You might try to write some on your own. . . . There's a prison paper you could contribute to."

"What's there to report, Dr. Brody? Ain't nothin' happenin' here. The news is on the outside where I can't get."

I was grateful to Superman (imagined paternal instrument of vengeance for oedipal wishes) for not having thrown Jesús off the roof. I'd have to keep a closer watch on Jesús.

"What do you think your real father was like?" I asked Jesús, hoping to find out what he had longed for . . . what he regarded as gratifying aspects of the father-child relationship: aspects he had been denied; first, because of his real father's disappearance before his birth, and subsequently by the unsatisfactory behavior of a step-father.

"My dad musta been the kind of guy didn' take shit from no one, especially no bimbos, and he make deals that put him on top. His clothes real fine, and he live good. We prob'ly go on vacation, like fishin' and climbin' mountains, and zip aroun' in his car. Well, he'd call me son, and he wouldn' hit me for nothin'! He the type that take me to Disney World. Mom said she think he do work there, but maybe not. She won't tell me his name. Now why she

73

throw him out? Why she fuckin' get rid of my dad? It a bad feelin'!"

"Are you angry?"

"I always angry, Doc. I angry when I sleep, and I angry when I jerk off. I angry when I eat, and I angry when I see other kids havin' a good time."

I was suspicious of the ease with which Jesús provided me with "hot" material. It was too accessible, too correct, and obviously designed to win my approval. He had picked up modes of behavior that only the experienced analysand could know (perhaps from previous encounters with members of my profession). It was a form of barter, and almost worthless . . . although what he made up might easily have been the truth (truth is also an invention, or at least a clever reconstruction).

Harry made it a habit to call me around eleven in the evening. I'm sure he wanted to interrupt me during some imagined sexual activity: masturbation or a quickie with an "Open til 12 A.M." pizza delivery person. He was bound to be disappointed since my spare time was spent, as usual, going over my notes or watching television. Harry preferred to believe that I kept my true self (more sensual . . . flagrantly voluptuous) for complete strangers, not for someone who was, as he thought of himself, as comfortable as an old slipper.

"You sound out of breath," Harry commented suspiciously.

"Out of breath?"

"Panting with desire would be more like it, Mathilda."

"I'm thinking, Harry. Thinking always excites me."

"About what, my darling? Would I be interested?"

"I'm glad you called, I need your opinion on something."

"Ask on."

74

"What effect do you think television violence has on the adolescent male? Do you think that watching TV can hypnotize the watcher and act in the same way as a drug?"

"How would I know, Mathilda?"

"Conjecture then; I'm interested in your opinion."

"This adolescent, is he usually a quiet guy, or someone who's angry all the time, ready to kick ass, has it in for the world?"

"Why, Harry?"

"I think the quiet guy would get his kicks just watching the violence, same as he would at the roller derby. Those people don't beat up on each other, or rob stores . . . they yell and throw things in the arena. It's a catharsis for them."

"And what about the angry person?"

"It just might get him cuckoo enough to go out and commit real violence. . . . Am I right?"

"I don't know . . . I was wondering about my patient; he's been exposed to hundreds of situations on TV where it's just as natural to shoot a person, bang-bang, as to eat a Carvel ice-cream sundae, yum-yum. . . . Now you take this kid, put a gun in his hand, put him into a situation where he is threatened, and what does he do?"

"He shoots."

"He's been conditioned to think that the proper thing for him to do is to shoot. He has no conscious awareness of what he is doing, but he has imagined himself doing this very thing many times. He has mentally rehearsed this action. Now you know that a rehearsal is preparation for performance . . . a rehearsal commits the mind and body to a fine-tuned readiness. . . ."

"Okay . . . so what's your opinion?"

"My opinion is that the trigger finger, as part of this emerging readiness, contracts reflexively over the trigger, and the gun goes off. The sad thing is, even though it is a conditioned reflex, I believe there is still awareness of what is happening."

"You talking about your patient?"

"Yes."

"He killed someone."

"Yes."

"I shouldn't have left you alone . . . I can move right back in."

"I told you I was safe."

"It's abnormal; it's bizarre . . . it's insane."

"I agree with you. There should be more research on the subject."

"I mean you, Mathilda . . . you're sacrificing yourself. You don't live a normal life."

"This is my work, and I love my work, Harry; you know that."

"But I miss you. You would have enjoyed the dinner I went to last night."

"Harry, I thought we'd decided never to say *would have, could have,* or *should have* to each other. Those burdensome words create guilt, and guilt kills . . ."

"Mathilda, I know you *would have* adored the steamed salmon, the puréed broccoli, the honeyed raspberry tart, and the conversation. My associate Tom Brockton actually confided to me that he had his secret lover delivered to him (he lives in a town house on Sutton Place) by dumbwaiter. . . . She must be small enough to ride on one of the shelves."

"Why are you telling me this, Harry? I'm losing my train of thought."

"I have a train of thought too, Mathilda, and talking on the phone with you has completely derailed me . . . I must see you."

"Why?"

"WHY!"

"Yes, why?"

"I'm about to attend an art conference in San Far-cisco . . . I mean San Francisco, and well, too much time away from you and I wander around like a lost person."

"All right . . . let's get together in a few days . . . I'll put it right here in my appointment book. . . . Ummm . . . Wednesday? Thursday?"

"Thursday evening . . . okay . . . I'll call to verify."

"Fine, darling."

"And I promise to be a good boy."

"What do you mean, Harry?"

"I'll avoid temptation in California, Mathilda . . . I wouldn't want to endanger our relationship."

"You'll do whatever you're going to do anyway, dear . . . besides, I don't care how you behave when you're away from me."

"You don't care? What if I meet someone so exciting in every way that you are eclipsed?"

"Can't get a rise out of me that way, Harry. Of course there are surprises out there; wonderful people you can have a great time with. Why should you deprive yourself . . . especially when I'll be occupied elsewhere."

"But, Mathilda, I depend on you to protect me from myself. . . . Other women frighten me . . . I, I don't do well with them. Stop me from going to the conference or I'll never speak to you again."

"I won't respond to blackmail, Harry. My advice is, face the danger. Pleasure is not lethal."

"How can you say that!"

"Harry, I'm sick and tired of hearing the Oepidus story. . . . Every woman is not your mother. If by some freak of nature you have fun in bed, your father, who has been dead these many years, will not come back to kill you; he'd be happy for you . . . and do not think that your childhood wish to see him dead actually caused his death. Go out and live, Harry, with my blessings!"

"Thank you, Mother! You always analyze things

away; however, *I* don't live by the analytic handbook, and *I* am the one who suffers from impotence."

"If you didn't I could never have stayed with you as long as I have. You give me a lot of space, darling. If you were any more demanding, my work would suffer."

"That's where it stands?"

"And, Harry, when you speak about receiving pleasure from women . . ."

"Yes?"

"Don't you mean men?"

# 8

_____

"You look very nice today, Allison; is that a new dress?"

"Actually no."

"I like the blue."

"Me too."

"So, how are you?"

"I didn't feel like coming today. I can't think of anything to say."

"Yes?"

"When I'm here it's as if I'm talking to the wall."

"What kind of wall?"

"What do you mean? A wall's a wall. It doesn't hear you. It stands in your way . . ."

"Do I look like a wall to you?"

Allison laughed. "No. Not really."

"Good. So why don't we think of what you can do to overcome what's in your way now."

"Remember last time, before I left, what I said?"

"What was that?"

"I told you I was lonely . . . so I tried to do something about it. I registered for a course in improvisation . . . even though I don't have any talent."

"Yes?"

"And it was fun . . . I pretended I was a washing machine . . . a front loader. Nobody could guess what I was. They thought I was a windmill. I should have been something easier, like a ball, or a rocking chair."

"But a washing machine is so original . . ."

"It wasn't my idea. Mr. Rueshames, the instructor, suggested it. He gave me three choices: ball, rocking chair, or washing machine. I also had my choice of speaking or not, but I couldn't bring myself to verbalize the inner thoughts of a washing machine: 'I go round and round . . . my cycles are numbered . . . nothing is too dirty for me.' Damn, you should have seen how clever the others were."

"This was the first time for you . . . next time you'll choose your own thing."

"There may never be a next time."

"Did you pay for the entire course?"

"Yes."

"Then take advantage of it . . . get your money's worth."

"I know I should, Dr. Brody, but I can't because of what happened. . . . Oh boy!"

"Couldn't be that bad."

"Yes, it was! I did something awful . . ."

"I'll get you some apple juice," I said. "Look at how beautiful the park is today." I drew the curtains. The park was a somber sight. It was already getting dark. "My mistake . . . it's a dismal day."

"I like it when it's quiet and gray. The sun only makes me feel worse." She paused and drew in her breath. "Oh God, he's followed me!"

"Who?"

"Mr. Rueshames. I see him down there by the bench. Look, he's putting his gloves into his pockets. Why would he do that? It's really cold outside. He must be coming into your building to wait for me."

I went to the window and did see a man below us, across the street. He looked familiar, but I couldn't place him. When had I met a Rueshames? Why was his name familiar?

"I'll bring you that apple juice, Allison," I said, "then we can talk about it. You're safe right now with me, aren't you?"

"Yes," she answered, "besides, it's not that he's dangerous or anything, it's just that . . . oh, I'll tell you later."

When I returned with the juice she was slumped in the chair opposite mine. "God, Dr. Brody, I hope he doesn't see me leaving. Is there another exit to this place?"

I assured her that she could use the service elevator. No one but delivery boys and the handyman ever used it, except in emergencies.

"Now . . . what's bothering you?"

"Well, it . . . well, what . . . this is what happened. I stayed after class and asked Mr. Rueshames whether or not I really had talent . . . whether he thought I should continue in his class. He invited me to have a beer with him at a bar . . . I was flattered . . . but actually he hadn't answered my question. He was teasing me, said that as soon as we were nice and cozy in the bar, he'd discuss it with me. Well, five beers later he still hadn't said a word to me about myself. Finally, I had to bring it up myself, I mean, it was very embarrassing. He said I should forget about trying to be an inanimate object and choose an exercise that involved the human experience. But he still hadn't told me whether or not I had any talent. So, I was very eager to find out. He was friendly . . . more than friendly. I found it difficult to think of him as my instructor. What kind of human experience should I work on? I asked. He urged me to drink more beer; to loosen up. I thought I'd pee in my pants . . . then he said he'd show me where his studio was, where he wrote his articles. I figured I could use the john there . . . so I didn't use the toilet in the bar. . . . I hate to use bar toilets, they're usually filthy. But he didn't have any toilet in his place . . . it was tiny . . . just enough room for a desk and a cot . . . there was a small sink in his room. I suppose the toilet was down the hall. I was on my knees on his cot looking out the window to see the view, when he, somehow, got under me and pulled my hip-huggers down . . . and he must have done something down there because I peed all over him . . . and you know something? He liked it! I just couldn't believe the reaction of the man. His shirt got soaked so he took it off and threw it on the floor. . . . He has a hole in his chest the size of a medium orange, and it's barely covered by a tiny tarpaulin of skin, like a pixie swimming pool. . . . He is disgusting, Dr. Brody, but he finally told me."

"Told you what?"

"That I had talent, but it would have to be developed. He gave me an exercise for our next class, the one I may not show up at."

"What's the exercise?"

"Leg wrestling . . . said if I did it good, he'd cast me in his documentary. He has a book out called *Relevance;* the one he's working on now is *The Naked Truth* . . . and the naked truth about me, Dr. Brody, is that I'm dirty! I'm dirtier than any toilet in a bar."

"Wash yourself," I said.

"Wash myself?"

"Then you won't feel dirty. I have patients who wash themselves constantly. It's the right thing to do."

"Dr. Brody, are you telling me that *you* think I'm dirty too?"

"No . . . I'm telling you that *you* think you're dirty."

"And I should wash?"

"Take a symbolic shower."

"How?"

"Don't get wet."

"You're wonderful, Dr. Brody; do you know what you've done?"

"What, Allison?"

"You've totally confused me. Is that good?"

"Only time will tell." I embraced her. That's what she really needed. That's what I wanted her to know, that words could go just so far, but an act of affection could say more than a thousand words.

"Thank you, Dr. Brody, but I still feel dirty . . . and I'm afraid . . . I'M AFRAID . . . I'M AFRAID . . . I'M AFRAID . . . I'M AFRAID . . . I'M AFRAID!" she screamed, over and over again, banging her hand on my desk. "I'M AFRAID!"

"I hear you. . . . You're not talking to the wall any more," I said, hugging her some more.

"Do you think I'll always be alone?" she sobbed. "I'm so lonely without Momma . . . and I haven't even told you about Papa."

"We'll deal with that next time. . . . Come, I'll help you to the elevator. . . . You can sneak out the back way."

After she had gone, I remembered where I had seen Mr. Rueshames; it had been on a TV interview, one of those public access channels, either J or K, a late evening show so casual that for a period of time during the interview no one realized that the guest was sitting on his microphone. Mr. Rueshames, when he could finally be heard, spoke about his dual careers as a writer on the drama and as an acting teacher. I noticed at the time that his voice had a phlegmy sound, as if it were struggling up from stagnant depths. At every opportunity during the interview he would boast about how much his students loved him, and how well attended his seminars were.

At the same time he had been doing something very odd; he had been collecting whatever sat on the table before him and putting these things into unusually capacious jacket pockets—the tiny crystal ashtray went in first, followed by a water glass, then two pencils (first toyed with innocently before entering his left pocket), after which he'd acquired a tiny, round, clip-on microphone, a man's handkerchief that had just left the hand of the host, some notepaper (crisply folded into squares), a reviewer's copy of his own book, some loose change, and a pair of the host's running shoes that he had hidden behind his chair. Obtaining the shoes had been more difficult than pocketing the smaller items; Mr. Rueshames had had to slide forward in his chair, then with the tip of one foot he had managed to snare the shoelaces (the shoes were tied together to enable the host to sling them over his shoulder) and drag the shoes over to his own chair. From there it had been simple to untie the laces and stuff a shoe into each pocket (thus giving him a uniformly hippy appearance). It was as if nothing unusual had transpired: Mr. Rueshames had even been invited back. Many of his students who were in the studio that night had reddened their palms with enthusiastic applause. I wondered whether this was really a take-off on a popular youth-oriented program, "Saturday Night Live," and whether the students had been applauding the professor's ostentatious and highly developed theatrical kleptomania, which was actually a master class in on-camera thievery.

The name Rueshames was especially revealing, I thought, both "rue" and "shame" having almost the same meaning. The name one inherits can be a cross to bear if one feels obliged to live up to it . . . or does fate give one a clue as to what is yet to come? It disturbed me that a man so mentally unbalanced should be so closely associated with impressionable young people, yet it was not up to me to take action; Allison would have to decide what to do.

# 9

## ALLENDEZ, JESÚS, FILE

This story on a young arsonist caused me to compare the crime of arson with the noncrime of enuresis; one sets the fires, the other puts them out. How are these two related? Both Jesús and the arsonist were rejected by their mothers (for other men); both Jesús and the arsonist had actual and imagined body defects: in the case of the arsonist an emaciated arm, a limp, and epilepsy; in the case of Jesús, his slow growth and small stature which caused him to regard himself as inferior to his peers. Both emulated superheroes, with the arsonist actually taking the name Bruce Lee (the late Kung Fu movie actor). Though the arsonist and Jesús chose heroes on the side of the law, they were compelled to break it.

### ARSONIST WHO KILLED 26 DRAWS LIFE TERM

Leeds, England (UPI)—Bruce Lee, a Bible-reading, partially crippled epileptic who caused the death of 26 persons in fires over the last seven years, was ordered yesterday to be confined for life in the huge kitchen of Trifles & Teacakes, HRM Co. where he will tend the old-fashioned, wood-burning stoves still in use there. The prosecuting advocate Mr. Hiram Greene said, "That oughta give him a taste of hell!" Lee is the worst mass killer in British criminal history.

Lee, 20, was ordered to the Park Lane special hospital near Liverpool, where he will undergo psychiatric treatment before taking up his duties as stoker and poker at the bakery. There had been some argument as to the correctness of the sentence, since it was thought that Mr. Lee, in light of his past and still active obsession with fire, might view his confinement with some pleasure. "We'll keep an eye on him," an official of the bakery union promised. "Temptation won't get the best of him this time. Give the lad a chance to prove himself."

In a confession read to the Leeds Crown Court, Lee admitted: "My fingers used to tingle when I was doing a fire. Whenever I had enough of people treating me like an animal I would just go out and set fire to a house." The advocate for the defense, obviously controlling his emotions, said: "If people had treated him like an animal he never would have done what he did. People love their animals and give them the best of care."

For nearly seven years, from the age of thirteen, Lee celebrated his puberty by starting fires in the northern English city of Hull, and only at his last fire, in which three young brothers died, did he leave any sign that it was not accidental . . . a box of unopened, blue birthday candles was found beside a box of partially used blue birthday candles. This enabled the police to trace the candles to the store in which they had been purchased, and consequently to the arsonist himself.

Only then did the police learn that seemingly unconnected fires in the city between 1973 and 1979 were the work of an arsonist. "He was a very clever chap," advocate Greene commented after wrapping up the case; "no two fires he set were alike . . . and he used modern methods to perpetrate the conflagration. The distorted use of an intelligence of this caliber is decidedly society's loss."

Lee pleaded guilty to 11 charges of arson and manslaughter between June 1973 and December 1979. His 26 victims ranged from a baby of six months to a man of 95. "I didn't want them to die," Lee said after the conviction; "homes should be fire-proofed so that people like me don't get funny ideas. They should have fire-drills too. Then they could get out."

Born Simon Pitticoe, the illegitimate son of a prostitute and an unknown father, he legally changed his name to that of the late Kung Fu movie actor Bruce Lee. He was born with a withered right arm, is epileptic, and limps from a spastic condition. At home he was sent into the street when his mother had a customer.

The previous worst mass killer in Britain was Mary Ann Cotton, hanged in Durham in 1873 for poisoning between 14 and 20 persons while employed as a hospital cook. She had regarded herself as a benefactor to mankind, chosen by God to put people out of their misery. Powerless to convince the court of her opinion, she had died proclaiming: "I am, I was, and always will be misunderstood!" Her victims were unable to take part in this debate.

What is it that the criminal wants us to understand?

"I called my mother," Jesús said, "she wants to bring me some flan. Can she come see me?"

"Soon," I promised.

"She said Al is sorry for what he done to me."

"What things?"

"When he hit me with his belt because of my report

87

card. . . . I don't care what he sorry for. . . . It too late to be sorry."

There could be no final resolution to his suffering if he did not forgive . . . or was he waiting for the *sorry* to be meant: proved in some other way than hearing it from his mother. What *did* Al's *sorry* mean? That it was hell at home now that Nina Allendez's boy had become a convicted murderer? That she would never forgive him for his role (explained to her by the court psychiatrists) in creating a monster (her son)? What else could the disciplinarian (Al) do, now that the effects of his discipline had proved deadly?

This Jesús could *not bring* the *dead* back to life. This Jesús was only able to *tread* water, *not walk* on it. This Jesús *threw* the *first stone*. This Jesús *turned* the other cheek only *to hide* his *anger*.

"Your mother would like you to forgive Al."

"Sure! But she still don't admit he's an asshole . . . thinks he's a great guy just because he say he sorry! Well, sayin' you're sorry is easy."

"Not for some."

"You on his side?" Jesús shouted. The intensity of his passionate nature was blunt and dangerous; real anger, not transference anger; I had become the enemy.

"I'm not defending him. I was generalizing."

"Well, Doc, don't ever generalize around me again. . . . It get me mad, and . . ."

"You're afraid you'll lose control?"

"Yeah."

"You're afraid you might hurt or kill me?"

"Hey, don't go putting ideas in my head. Shit!"

"It's okay for you to get mad."

His distress coincided with emotional rigidity on my part. I had been frightened and suppressed it. Raissa had only growled a few times in response to our raised voices,

88

and then gone back to her nap. It was okay for Jesús to get mad . . . but not too mad.

For our second video session, Jesús chose the scene at the station house where he had been booked.

"All right, we're in the station house now," I said, entering the imaginative territory of my patient.

"Shit, what gonna happen to me now?" Jesús asked.

"Allendez, here's a card for you to read. Make sure you understand what it says."

"What it say, Officer?"

"It says that you have the right to remain silent and to consult an attorney."

"Would you please ask my parents to leave the room."

I spoke to the make-believe parental figures. "Mr. and Mrs. Allendez, would you please wait outside, while I interrogate the suspect?"

The figures left the office.

Jesús leaned forward, a willing witness against himself. "Look, I did it and I just want to tell you about it. I just want to get it off my chest."

"I'm not coercing you. You are about to offer this information of your own free will?"

"Yes, sir."

"And when you are done, are you willing to sign the transcript of your confession?"

"Yes, sir . . . only . . ."

"Only what, Allendez?"

"Only I don't want to say I."

"You have to say I, if it's a confession."

"I want to say he . . . like telling a story . . . it's easier."

"But this he will be you?"

"The he will be I."

"Try it, Jesús."

89

# HIS CONFESSION BY JESÚS ALLENDEZ

He knew that there was a dance planned at the school that evening, and he needed money. He knew that sometimes Mrs. Kent left her door unlocked when she left the house, and he knew that she had gone shopping. He went into the side door of the house that opens into the kitchen and began looking through the house for money. He found an envelope on a closet shelf that contained a lot of money. He took it. He found a revolver in a dresser drawer. While he was in the bedroom Mrs. Kent came home. She caught him. She said, I know you, you're Jesús Allendez, the boy I thought was my friend. He told her he didn't steal anything. He asked her not to call the police. She said she'd have to. He said, Don't. He said he needed the money to go to the dance at school and for a good time. She said, I won't tell if you dance with me. I'm a good dancer. I have good records here. She danced all around. She was old and ugly. She grabbed his arm. Dance with me. Dance with me, she said. She acted crazy. He said, I don't dance with old ladies. She stopped dancing and went to the telephone. He pointed the gun at himself. Stop, he said, or I'll do this to you. I'll shoot you in your stomach. She said, I'll tell your mother. I'll call the police. I'll send a telegram to Kojak. The gun pointed at her. It went off before he knew it. She sat on the floor. I guess I danced too much, she said, would you bring me a glass of whiskey and water from the kitchen? He went to the kitchen, found the bottle of whiskey, poured her a drink and brought it back to her. He handed her the drink. She fell over backward, and spilled the drink on herself. He asked her if she was dead. She didn't get up after that. Then he went through the house and wiped his fingerprints off of everything he had touched before. He took the car keys that she had left on the table in the hall when she came in. He put her TV into the car. Then he got into the car and left.

Signed: Jesús Allendez
Sworn to Be the Truth: Jesús Allendez
HE: JESÚS ALLENDEZ

"So that's your story, and you're going to stick to it?"
"Yes, Officer."
"Haven't you left something out?"
"No."

He refused to mention the rape. His story had been curiously emotionless. The rage had burned itself out. Using he instead of I had given him the distance he needed; the authority to edit the material.

"I look bigger on TV," Jesús noted, "so do you . . . but not as big as the real detective who book me . . . he was over six feet tall. Put me in a cage right there in the office. He didn't smile like Merv Griffin. Maybe Tom Snyder on the 'Tomorrow' show is taller than that detective. I saw him stand up next to Mickey Rooney. Donahue is taller than Merv Griffin and Dick Cavett, but he's shorter than Tom Snyder. They're all the same sitting down. If I was invited on a show I'd be sitting down. But Dick Cavett wouldn't invite me to be his guest because I don't sit still and I'm not the most famous criminal. Maybe if he has a crime expert on with me it be okay. Donahue could do it up good with you, Dr. Brody, and he could invite some members of my family and the victim family and some other psychiatrist who disagree with you. He like to give his audience the full picture. He let them ask questions, like 'Do you believe in capital punishment?,' 'What the chances are that this punk ain't gonna go out and do it again?,' 'Is this rehabilitation program a gross misuse of taxpayers' money?' Hey, Doc, my face is orange. Can't you adjust the color?"

"No, I can't. It's a cheap old set . . . and something's wrong with the film too. . . . Say, you mentioned capital punishment; do you believe in it? Would it have deterred you from crime?"

He became coy, and played with me, perhaps to allay anxiety. "How you gonna punish the Capitol? It just a place in Washington, D.C. Or do you mean it the big letter at the beginning of a sentence like they teach in school? If you punish that big-shit letter that lead all the rest you gonna have to cut it down to size so it look like all them baby letters runnin' around the page, and there be confusion in alphabet land."

"Don't be a smart-ass. You know what capital punishment is!"

"No I don't . . . tell me."

"The death sentence for murderers."

"Do that mean I'd be dead and gone right now if it was the law?"

"Yes."

"I'm against it."

"You'd rather live and suffer?"

"Where there's life there's hope, Doc. Damn right!"

"Don't say damn, Allendez."

"Sorry, but you got me all steamed."

"Go make yourself some lunch. . . . You're being a pain in the ass."

"You don' have nothin' I like to eat," he complained. "I hate melted cheese sandwiches and chicken noodle soup. How come you don't never put no garlic in your food? And I never see rice and beans in my plate. How come? You got food prejudice?"

"Why don't you write a list of foods you'd like and I'll call the order in."

"You're supposed to be smart," he continued in an argumentative tone, "but even the records you have suck! Ever heard of Chick Corea? Ever listen to Latino music? To salsa?"

"No."

"Somethin' missing from your education. . . . What you doin' with me? How you gonna understand me? I ain't just anybody. I'm Jesús Allendez. Think about it."

"Say, what are you up to, Jesús?"

"I just want to make sure I get the best possible treatment." He sauntered away, confident that he held the upper hand. "You think I ain't got no choice, but I do. I can stay here and be your guinea pig, or I can go back to jail where I know what's what, or I can take off . . ."

"You don't mean that?"

"Don't I?"

I did not use the confidential information against him that I had received from Dr. Menninger Hong-Harvey concerning his degrading sexual experience at the facility. I knew he would never, voluntarily, return there.

"I hope you decide to stay," I said, "for my sake as well as for yourself."

"What you mean by your sake?" There was a note of caution in his voice; something hoped for but not able to be expressed . . . a longing for love? Was I reading into it? I realized that I had a similar need . . . I wanted him to love me, his jailer.

"You're growing on me, kid," I said. "I like having you around."

He responded by putting his arms around me. "Thanks, Doc. I really appreciate that. I do."

One of several channels leading directly to the problem of a distorted self had opened up. Specific pockets of discontent would still have to be gone through, their contents emptied and sorted out . . . things of value saved.

That evening, when Jesús had trouble falling asleep I gave him a massage. His body hadn't been touched for such a long time (we forget that the body has to be touched); I kneaded the tense knots, smoothed them out, stroked his back till he fell asleep under my hands. As I drew the covers up over him, I thought, If only his destiny were not bound entirely by his primitive (if recent) past, he'd have a chance.

"Don't tell me about the demanding minutiae of your diurnal and nocturnal jottings, Mathilda! I fully expected us to get together before I leave, and you did not call me!

Don't you consult your appointment book? I expect you never intended to call me."

"Simmer down, Harry, I simply forgot."

"Simply? My dear, one forgets what one wants to forget. You told me that yourself."

"I'm too tired to argue. Forgive me? You always have. . . . I do love you, you know that."

"Do you remember the last time we spoke?"

"Vaguely."

"I mentioned the steamed salmon . . . come, come, you do remember the fish, don't you?"

"Not really. What about the steamed salmon?"

"Well, of course, not really; at the time I mentioned it you showed no interest in the meal . . . how it was served . . . who was there."

"Harry, is there a story connected to the steamed salmon you think I'd enjoy? If there is, tell it to me; don't ask permission."

"Do you regard the complete ravishing of a gourmet dish by two Maltese cats set loose upon a banquet table by the host an enjoyable story?"

"Did the cats' feast deprive you of your main course, dear?"

"It deprived me of my appetite, even though the dish of steamed salmon was instantly replaced by another exactly like the first."

"You must choose your friends more carefully. Was that your friend's idea of a practical joke?"

"Lanyard is known for his 'jokes.' "

"Sadism, you mean. My dear, one's guests should never be made to wait an inordinate amount of time for their dinners. Is that the end of your story? I'd like to have your opinion on a question that concerns me a hell of a lot more than what your society friends are doing to amuse themselves."

"You don't want to hear it!"

"Yes, I do."

"It's bound to upset you."

"Isn't that why you want me to hear it? Oh, go on!"

"Lanyard planted trees on his terrace . . ."

"What's upsetting about that?"

"During the dessert he opened the blinds . . ."

"Now that's cruel."

"And hanging from the branches of a tree . . . sparkling among the branches was . . ."

"A stalactite?"

"A dead dog. Its head was lifted by a rope, and had stiffened in that position. I thought it was a conceptual piece that Lanyard had acquired for his collection. It was the family dog!"

"What did you do about it, Harry?"

"Nothing, Mathilda . . . the dog was already dead. Lanyard's promised to sell the museum a good portion of his collection, can't afford to anger him . . . though heaven knows, the man deserves the death penalty himself!"

"Which brings me to what I want to question you about, darling. Do you believe in capital punishment?"

"Of course not, Mathilda. I don't believe in the taking of one life for another."

"What about society's need for revenge?"

"It's a need that can't be satisfied. Kill one murderer and ten spring up in his place. Society has to be changed. It's an economic problem, as you well know, Mathilda."

"But you said that Lanyard deserves the death penalty."

"Just letting off steam. However, if the murderer is not able to be rehabilitated, I do believe in the release and stalk method."

"What is that? Haven't heard of it."

"The convicted, incorrigible murderer is released

and then an execution squad is assigned to track him down. This way, the murderer is forced to experience the same kind of terror that his own victim or victims felt before he killed them."

"You're speaking of revenge, Harry. You've reversed your opinion in about two seconds. . . . Is this what you'd like to happen to Lanyard?"

"Frankly, yes."

"Was the dinner a degrading experience for you?"

"It was."

"In what way did it degrade you?"

"I was made a fool of."

"In what way do you think you were made a fool?"

"The others at the dinner table regarded me as a coward and therefore an inferior person."

"Were you an inferior person when you arrived at dinner?"

"Of course not."

"Weren't you the same person during dinner?"

"Yes."

"My dear, you are a human being, and as such you are what you are. What do you think happened to you at the dinner? Did you lose an arm or a leg?"

"No."

"So, even physically you remained the same. Don't you understand that nobody can lower your self-esteem if you won't let them?"

"I'm too sensitive."

"Yes, you are . . . and too timid. Next time do not preoccupy yourself with a fear of the consequences; act on your righteous hostilities. You were upset by that dead dog!"

"Yes, I was. I tried to put it out of my mind but I couldn't."

"I understand. Try to learn from your mistakes, Harry, express yourself next time."

"I'm still hostile to you, Mathilda."

"Good."

"You're a bitch, Mathilda!"

"If I am, then I am . . . but I've never been a prolonged bitch. . . . Why don't you call me when you return from California?"

"Because I'm not going to California. I've decided against it. I'm needed here to help Tom with the Katmandu show."

"Have it your own way."

"I'll try. . . . Look, I'll call you again in a few days when things get back to normal here . . . if they ever do. Here's a big kiss for you."

"Not hostile any more?"

"Can't afford to be."


## MISCELLANEOUS FILE

### ON THE HOUSEKEEPING OF VIOLENCE: MESSY OR NEAT

"Spontaneous" violence is baroque (seldom romantic), it is performed in a rush; the scene of the crime left in passionate disorder. This is messy housekeeping.

Suppressed rage creates the methodical killer, the murderous holder of a grudge, e.g., the suicide. As the suicide thumbs his bloody nose at those who will find him, he is saying: "See, even in death I take care of myself. My life did not touch you and now my death will not." He is usually a citizen concerned with neat housekeeping. There have been two recent examples of this latter method: one, a well-known female photographer who lay down in her bathtub before cutting her wrists. The blood disappeared down the drain. The other, a male artist, had rested his wrist, soft side up, in the basin of his studio sink before slitting it. The blood disappeared down the drain, leaving only a few smudges on the porcelain surface of the sink.

Neither of these people wanted their blood touched. Selfish to the end. Or should I say sensitive?

Jesús Allendez was a poor housekeeper . . . he created a mess . . . then left things as they were. I would, perhaps, take some pills, then drift off forever, closing my mind, which is where I live.

# 10

The phone rang. I listened in as the tape recorded the caller, ready to speak if it was someone I wanted to respond to; it was. Allison, her speech lazy and slurred, had called to say goodbye!

"Where are you going?" I asked, alarmed.

"To hell," she said. "I called to say goodbye. So goodbye."

"Did you take something, Allison?"

"My Valiums. . . . I want you to know I really love you, Dr. Brody, but it just won't work any more . . . it isn't your fault."

"I'll be right over," I shouted. "Try to vomit . . . put your finger down your throat and get it all up. Do it! Go on!"

I hung up and caught a cab going uptown to Washington Heights. The super let me into the Kent apartment. Allison was on the floor between two beds, the phone cradled in her lap, its curling umbilical cord dangling from the telephone table above.

"I can't go with you," she announced, "I've got to find my wallet."

"You don't need it!" I tugged at her, trying to raise her up.

"I do," she cried. "Momma's picture is in it."

"Forget it!" I ordered.

The super helped me carry her out, scratching and kicking. For someone half-conscious, she exerted a stubborn strength.

In the cab she punched me in the teeth. "We'll be there soon," I said, touching my lips to see if they were bleeding. A tiny trickle of blood was coming from the lower lip where a tooth had cut it. Getting out of the cab at the Columbia Presbyterian Medical Center's emergency room, I had to drag her, legs dangling, bare feet scraping along the driveway, into the reception area. By this time she had passed out.

After two hours (she had been whisked away from me to be examined, and her stomach pumped), an orderly appeared, wheeling her down the hall in a wheelchair. A doctor, who was not sure whether she should be admitted to their psychiatric division, asked her some questions: "Do you know what today is? What day is today?"

"Today I wrote a poem," Allison answered in a tired voice.

"Then you don't know what today is?" he said. "What month is it, then? Do you know what month it is?"

"It's the Year of the Monkey," she said confidently. "In the Year of the Rat we moved to the city."

"Is she hallucinating?" the doctor asked me. He didn't even know who I was. How would any ordinary citizen know whether someone was hallucinating?

I answered him, "No, she is not. She had dinner in Chinatown with friends this evening and is referring to the Chinese calendar." I invented this, of course.

"Is she a Chinese scholar?" He looked at her with new respect and not as if she were a nut case, then, sud-

100

denly curious about me, asked, "Are you related to Ms. Kent?"

"I'm her doctor," I answered, reluctant to admit that I was her shrink. Look at where it had gotten her.

His attitude changed. "The Valiums were bad enough, but the monosodium glutamate didn't help either," he confided. "She probably suffered an allergic reaction to the stuff."

"You can release her in my care," I said, "she'll be okay now."

After signing some papers, she was mine. We were in a cab again, when she said, "I need slippers." She took a size nine, and her favorite color was yellow, preferably terry-cloth. We stopped at two drugstores and one small shoestore before finding her a pair of cherry-colored velvet flip-flops one size too small (her heels extended beyond the open backs). She didn't like them.

"You're not in a fashion show," I pointed out, "you can take them off when we get home."

"Home?"

"My home, Allison, I want to keep an eye on you, and I have to be at home."

"My feet are the nicest part of me," she said, "but they're so far away, I can't see them. Why are they at the bottom, and I'm at the top? Answer me that. Mr. Rueshames says I have a beautifully curved instep like a dancer. He wants to measure my calves for a scientific survey he's taking. Oh, I can't stand intellectual men!" She dozed off and on while I tried to keep her talking. I did not relish the prospect of dragging her into the lobby by myself. I had done enough lugging of human baggage for one night.

"Mr. Rueshames is superficially erudite," I informed her; "he's not a real intellectual."

"He's not?"

"No, he's not. He's a run-of-the-mill pedant."

101

"You're wrong," she said, "he likes women."

I held my tongue; it was a moot question whether or not a man who fears women as much as Mr. Rueshames obviously did could like them. Allison had confused the meaning of pederasty with the lesser evil of pedantry. Pederasty was at the bottom, while pedantry lived upstairs. Both subjects were pedestrian to me, of no particular interest since my research (categorically) lay elsewhere. However, when I thought about it again, there *was* some connection, the stem *ped.*

Allison was tucked into bed in the small study just off the waiting room. It was quiet in there, cut off from the rest of the house.

The next morning, Allison was still asleep when I went in to check on her. Her breathing was regular, her color good, and so I did not wake her before going to the post office to pick up a parcel. The housekeeper knew she was in there, and had orders not to disturb her. Only Jesús did not know I had an overnight guest. . . . I expected to return in time to speak to Allison, and to direct the household traffic so that Allison and Jesús would not meet. By the time I returned, Allison had gone. Among my messages on the phone tape was the communication that she (Allison) would resume sessions with me, usual time, in two days . . . and that she hadn't really wanted to die. She thanked me for saving her, and then I heard a loud crack in my ear; she had sent me a kiss through the receiver.

"You know that Rousseau with the lion and the sleeping woman?" Allison asked.

"No."

"I saw it at the Modern . . ."

"Oh, yes." I did not correct Allison. The woman in the Rousseau painting, *The Sleeping Gypsy,* was a man.

"It upset me."

"Why?"

102

"Was the woman dead?"

"What do you think?"

"You know how dogs don't leave their masters if they're dead? Well, I think the woman is dead and the faithful lion is standing watch over her."

"Possible. How did the woman die?"

"Uh-oh . . . here we go."

"What do you mean, 'Here we go'?"

"Someone raped the woman. . . . It's not a peaceful scene."

"No."

"She was surprised by a rapist. . . . Where'd you go when I stayed over? I woke up and you were gone."

"Had to sign for a package at the post office. I expected to see you when I got back."

"Didn't feel like waiting. You should have left me a note. Anyway, I left in such a hurry that I forgot my purse . . . so I came back to the apartment . . . you still weren't there. The housekeeper let me in."

"I'm sorry I missed you. You should have waited."

"Well, I should have but I didn't. . . . I got upset . . . oh, hell!"

"Why did you get upset?"

"I saw Jesús Allendez. He was in the kitchen making his breakfast just like an ordinary person! He smiled at me and I started to get sick. I couldn't stop shaking."

"Did he recognize you too?"

"No, I don't think so. . . . He asked me did I want some crazy eggs? He was putting ketchup all over the eggs; it looked like blood."

"It does look like that."

"And then the housekeeper came in. She made a fresh pot of coffee and offered me a cup, which I took. The murderer sat opposite me at the table."

"You faced him; you were that close? Did you say anything?"

103

"I was confused . . . the situation was so weird."

"You internalized."

"My stomach was turning; I did manage to say, 'How could you?' He didn't know what I was talking about. He asked me if I was a friend of yours. I suppose he didn't remember me from the courtroom; his eyes were always looking down."

"And then?"

"I did a cowardly thing; I pretended to accidentally spill my hot coffee. It wet his lap and burned him. The housekeeper wiped it up. If only I'd had a gun."

"What did Jesús do?"

"He said, 'Bitch!' "

"Oh . . ."

"He left the room. Then I went to the museum. That night I dreamed that the lion was Raissa, and I was the dead woman in the desert. Jesús raped me. . . . Tell me, does that rat sleep good at night?"

"No better than you do."

"There's something I haven't told you, Dr. Brody . . . ever since I was a teenager . . . well, I used to imagine I was raped; and I liked it . . . it was exciting . . . I used to think about how I'd be interviewing some men for a job, and this handsome man, sometimes Hispanic, sometimes black, would come in and make me take my clothes off, and rape me on the office floor. He wouldn't hurt me or anything . . . just force me to have intercourse . . . just lie there without making any sounds while he did whatever he did, you know."

Allison's masturbation fantasy was not an uncommon one; it was indicative of the innate masochistic component revealed often enough in the female sex. It is harmless and does not mean that an actual rape might be welcome. Besides the sexual pleasure it allows, it pacifies the actual fear of such a thing happening, by pretending that it is desirable. It also renders the female dreamer guiltless since she is unable to prevent the sexual act from occurring—a no-blame situation. However, such fantasies indulged in by Allison after her mother's rape and murder *would* create enormous guilt in her (the mother was an actual victim). In her own mind, Allison would then become an accessory to the crime, if she did nothing to avenge it . . . if she purposely cohabited with the murderer! (I notice I have used the word "actual" three times to prove to myself [1] that rape is real; [2] that fear is real; [3] that being a victim is real.) Rousseau's *The Sleeping Gypsy* is not real. It is a contact dream (like a "contact high," as Jesús would say). The gypsy, whom Allison made into a woman (into herself/her mother) has a swarthy complexion . . . the men in Allison's fantasy are all of an opposite ethnic persuasion: black or Hispanic . . . the incorporation of prejudice (fear of *the other*, the *stranger*) into a neat little package of pleasure? But this is another line of inquiry. It will all come out in the wash: the blood, the dirt, the money forgotten in a pocket. . . . The wash-analysis.

"It's perfectly all right to have fantasies," I said stupidly. "What if you had no imagination?"

"Then things would be the way they are," Allison answered.

"Things are never the way they are," I countered, hoping she would not challenge me, and make me spend the rest of the hour giving examples.

"No, they aren't," she responded. "Even my father was not the man he seemed to be. He was a great pretender."

"Your father?"

From a photograph of Allison's father, I created a mask resembling him.

"Why are you wearing that mask?" Allison asked.

"Isn't it familiar to you?"

105

"Should it be?"

"There's a family resemblance."

"What family?"

"Yours."

"Mine?"

"It won't help you to deny that this is a likeness of your father."

"It's not . . . it looks like a death mask."

Out of a need to deny to herself that her father was dying, Allison had not told him that she loved him . . . nor did she have the opportunity to hear him say that he loved her. On this count she had sought constant reassurance from me that she was indeed a person worthy of affection, and that I would not abandon her as her parents had. During an effective session she was able to recall sexual feelings she had had as a child while sitting on her father's lap, and nonsexual feelings (nonconflicted) while sitting on her mother's lap (occurring soon after the father had left the family).

Bypassing the appropriate behavior of an analyst, I allowed Allison, large as she was, to sit on my lap in order to attenuate realistic, affectionate, nonsexual loving feelings . . . to let her experience again the mutual love that existed between herself and her mother.

Memories of her mother's emotional warmth emerged in terms of her requests for food she had been given as a child: orange juice, milk, junket, tapioca, Cream of Wheat.

She remembered that she had brought her father a piece of cake wrapped in Saran Wrap (at the hospital where he lay dying) and that he had bitten into it without removing the wrapper.

"They took his teeth away," she said, "so he wouldn't eat. I fed him orange sherbet. He didn't need teeth for that."

"No."

106

"They were supposed to take him for walks down the hall. They didn't. They put him in a chair and left him till he dirtied himself; then they cleaned him up and put him back in bed. Little by little everything was taken away from him. . . ."

Based on Allison's feelings for her father, I chose appropriate music for the waiting room (when she was expected) titled "Dance of the Grieving Child" (music inspired by a Paul Klee painting). At first Allison sat very still, deep in her own thoughts, but then, after a frame of five or six measures, when a veil of sound fluttered apart revealing a dreamlike waltz movement, she rocked back and forth. This waltz reminded Allison of when she had danced with her father, stood on his shoes as he waltzed her around.

At every hesitation (musical), recovery (beat), and dissonance (chord), I expected Allison to cry out, or sing a few notes . . . to make some rasping or mournful sound . . . but there was nothing . . . only the autistic rocking back and forth, the rhythm of an infant banging its head against the bars of its crib. The melody went on, sounding transparent, shatterproof keys, until with a few ascending lines of airy arpeggio it ended.

"That music . . ." Allison said.

"Yes?"

"Reminds me of . . . oh, it hurts so much to remember."

"Yes."

"I was a little girl in love with her father."

"And what else, what else? Why are you so frightened of masks?"

Allison stared at me. "Masks? When have we discussed masks?"

"We haven't, but your reaction a few sessions ago . . . when I put on a mask. . . ."

"Oh, yes . . . yes, yes, yes. You're right . . . I have a fear of masks, but I've masked it . . . perhaps a lifetime fear . . . a visit to Lamston's around Halloween used to terrify me: the witch masks, the monsters . . ."

"You have a fear of masks? Or of masklike faces? Tell me, Allison, what is a mask?"

"A mask is put on to hide one's identity. Its expression is frozen . . . somewhere behind the mask the real face is trapped and will never be seen again. It is a terrible shock to encounter its substitution, the mask."

"What if the mask is not a substitution?"

"I don't know."

"May I suggest that as a child it was you who discovered someone very close to you, dead . . . that the loved one's face, formerly mobile and full of life, had become a mask?"

"I don't remember, and there is no one left to ask. No one who might have found a child crying beside a loved one who would not awaken."

"Your *not* remembering is so explicit, Allison; you are beginning to remember. . . . Let's not push it for now."

# 11

---

"Your friend was here the other day," Jesús said. "I told her you be right back . . . but she couldn't wait."

"Did you ask her name?"

"No . . . I offer her some eggs, my specialty; she say no, and then she spill her hot coffee in my lap! I run outta the kitchen before I kill again. Man, she sure clumsy . . . but she kinda foxy, remind me of someone, some star, I dunno."

"She's Allison Kent."

"What she doin' here in your house? How come she didn't get her revenge on me?"

"The housekeeper let her in, she forgot something."

"Yeah, she forgot to kill me, that's what! I ain't safe here. I gotta go."

"Hold it . . . she's one of my patients and she didn't have you in mind at all."

"She spill hot coffee on me. It burn my leg. It all red. Maybe it be infected and I die in a few days."

"You're okay . . ."

"No, I'm not. I don't feel secure no more."

"She won't sleep over again. There were special circumstances."

"She slept over! Wow! I bet she look at me sleepin'. I bet she see my naked body and all, and curse the shit outta me."

"I don't think so."

"Yeah, I bet she couldn' take her eyes off of me."

"It won't happen again. . . . She won't stay over."

It has been said that the eye is the window to the soul, but I say that the eye *is* the soul, and not merely a transparent barrier that keeps the soul locked within the head. Both light and emotion cause the eye (soul) to react. . . . The eye as well as the mouth belongs to the oral stage (taking things in), thus the expression of a lover to his loved one that "I could eat you up with my eyes," or "Let me feast my eyes on you." In a dream that Jesús had, he was prevented from seeing, when the bars of his (dream) cell turned into devouring teeth. What he had been looking at is, of course, of prime importance . . . but he couldn't remember. May I suggest the primal-scene, with Jesús himself incestuously engaged?

The stimulus properties of pictures is useful in extricating buried material from a patient; it reveals his attitude toward the illustrated situation. Naturally this varies from patient to patient. I selected some cards for Allison, and some for Jesús. The Jesús session came first.

1. *Description:* On the floor against a couch is the huddled form of a boy with his head bowed on his right arm. Beside him on the floor is a revolver.

2. *Manifest Stimulus Demand:* a. The huddled form of a person, generally seen as young, of either sex. The figure is in a

situation of a negative character calling for some explanation.

b. Other details consist of the object on the floor, most generally seen as a gun or other weapon. It is entirely possible, however, to see this as another object (a bunch of keys, for example) without distortion. The "couch" itself is often mentioned though seldom plays a central part in the story.

3. *Form Demand:* The figure and the "gun" are the only two forms of importance. It would appear that roughly one-fourth to one-third of subjects concern themselves in some way with the object on the floor, whether seeing it as a gun, or other object, or merely indicating awareness of it without identifying it.

4. *Latent Stimulus Demand:* The picture presents a lone figure in what is generally a negative circumstance. Unless the story is unusually logically constructed it would be expected to be negative in quality. It is a stimulus saying to the subject: What could he be expected to do about it? As such, it arouses associations of loss, guilt, attack, and aggression. It is important that this is a lone figure and hence attitudes toward the isolated self tend to be aroused.

5. *Frequent Plots:* The stories usually deal with a person who has been attacked or who is himself guilty about his own misdemeanor.

6. *Significant Variations:* The "gun" is perhaps the most important single point for special attention. There is some tendency to think that it can readily lend itself to symbolic statements of sexual concern or be intentionally ignored in a story that could readily have utilized it.

The day after his chance encounter with Allison, Jesús was unresponsive. "I just gonna sit here and watch TV. I gonna watch 'Family Feud' . . . that guy who run the show, he get to kiss all the girls. . . . Man, is he ugly!"

"You're falling right back into a self-destructive pattern again, Jesús! I want that set off!"

"So what I got to do? Nobody here kissin' *me,* or givin' *me* a chance to win the big money. I sure am useless."

"I'll play a game with you."

"Yeah? You gonna test my intelligence? You gonna be disappointed."

"Look at this picture."

"What I supposed to see?"

"Whatever's there. Tell me what you see."

"Okay . . . there's this guy on the floor and he's cryin' so he hide his face. He got his gun on the floor next to him what he bought on the street. He don't know what to do. Shoot hisself? That ain't his couch. That somebody else's couch in somebody else's house. It old and got a hole covered up. Well, a old lady put some money in that hole, and he got the money. The main thing is, he didn't know it, but he twist his foot and can't get up. So even if he decide to blow hisself away, he can't reach the gun. He lonely and sick waitin' for the cops. When they find him, he gonna clam up. So his one good idea backfired and he spend the rest of his days behind bars. Not because of the money he stole, but the old lady's corpse is under the couch. And he hear her yellin' in his head. And he smell her body 'cause it been under the couch for two days."

"Would you say that the boy in the picture was a victim himself?"

"I would say he weren't too cool and that he should've crawl outta there and save hisself."

"But he doesn't."

"He can't. The dumb jerk he sprain his ankle . . . and besides he got this feelin' that he don't care anyway."

"Then why is he crying?"

"His foot hurt."

112

"Is that the only reason?"

"Maybe he feel he went too far without meanin' to
. . . when he lose his cool his anger jump out, and without
his anger he get weak and scared again, and he give up."

"Will he ever forgive himself ?"

"I hope so. . . . He too young to fall apart."

Keeping Jesús with me, without friends he could relate to, was not a healthy situation for either of us. . . . If
he hadn't already been ill, he most certainly would have
begun to display symptoms typical of prisoners who suffer
sensory deprivation. And if I hadn't been so affectionate,
behaving in ways he wanted his parents to behave to him
(at certain stages of his development) he would once again
have become Superman, or Kojak, identity models who
were able to defend themselves and others . . . and who
*deserved* love because of their extraordinary attributes.
An ordinary human being who needs love and does not
get it is at a decided disadvantage, and blames *himself* for
the rejection. I wanted Jesús to feel safe with me; however, a jealous bureaucracy (that cared more for its statis-
tics than people's lives) could snatch him away from me
at any time. I needed at least four more years with Jesús
before his analysis could be called a success. Early glean-
ings showed that he was trying to open up emotionally,
that he was beginning to like himself, e.g., his response to
the testing card, when I'd asked "Will he ever forgive
himself ?" and he'd answered, "I hope so. . . . He too
young to fall apart." Jesus regarded me as having power
in the world, of being able to influence those who had
power over him, therefore, if he was taken back to prison,
his disillusion would be complete: he'd blame me. "Why
wasn't Dr. Brody able to protect me?" he'd ask himself,
and the answer might be, according to the way he regarded himself, "Because she doesn't really want me. She
doesn't care about me. She doesn't love me!" Once Jesús

113

Allendez convinced himself of these thoughts, he'd swiftly become, once again, a danger to himself or others.

The thing for me to do, as I always have, is to work against time.

## KENT, ALLISON, FILE

Results of descriptive card #5: Test given to Allison Kent, post suicide attempt.

1. *Description:* A middle-aged woman is standing on the threshold of a half-open door looking into a room.

2. *Manifest Stimulus Demand:* a. An adequate accounting will refer to the woman and some explanation of why she is entering the room.
b. Other details often noted are the objects in the room. Not infrequently figures are introduced, normally seen as in the room portrayed.

3. *Form Demand:* The form of this picture lends itself to special preoccupation with minor details. Generally, however, the task is simple, set by the two large details of the woman and the room.

4. *Latent Stimulus Demand:* This is a picture especially likely to portray attitudes toward the maternal figure, especially when seen as prohibitive and supervisory. In adolescents particularly, the apprehension of adult control of sexual explorations is often brought out.

5. *Frequent Plots:* The woman is usually seen as having surprised someone in the room or as having heard something which she comes to investigate.
NOTE: A similar picture used for the cover of a "juvenile" novel, *Ghost House* . . . a tale of three terrified kiddies . . . a tot peering apprehensively through a half-open door is set against a white (neutral) background. Instead of con-

veying evil, brooding houses, or sinister fogs, the book
company shows frightened innocents. . . . A partial quote
from a book editor is to the point: ". . . Any good horror
story preys on *primal terror.*"

6. *Significant Variations:* A special point of interest here lies in
the problem or persons in the room. It not infrequently
occurs that some voyeuristic tendencies are displayed
through the woman not announcing herself. Similarly, apprehension over possible maternal (?) punishment results
in denial of all affect and emphasis merely upon inspection
of the contents of the room. It is possible for the scene
behind the room to be brought into the story.

Allison turned the picture around and around as if
she couldn't tell what was up and what down. "What's the
trick?" she asked. "Am I supposed to find sixteen things
that are wrong with this picture?"

"No. Just make up a story about what you see."

"The drawing is terrible," she said. "The artist can't
draw."

"That isn't what matters."

"Well, there's more than one story in that picture . . . don't you think so?"

"I agree."

"The woman standing at the door to the bedroom is
really a child dressed in her mother's leopard-skin hat.
She's playing dress-up."

"The room is a bedroom, then?"

"I think so . . . yes, it is. . . . The child who is in the
picture is playing dress-up in her own room nearby when
she hears arguing between her parents. She opens the
door to their room a crack. Her father, who is very angry
at her mother for something, slams the door and it hits the
little girl in the head. Her head begins to bleed and she
has to be taken to the hospital for stitches. She still has the
scar on her forehead."

Allison lifted the hair from her forehead, and there, barely perceptible, was a narrow, pod-shaped scar in the center. "I'm told it can be removed," she said.

"What do you think your parents were arguing about?"

"I know what they were arguing about because Momma told me years later, but at the time I thought it was because I had been naughty, and Daddy was defending me, and Momma was blaming me. Of course I had it all wrong. Daddy was mad at Momma because she was having an affair with someone else and I just happened to be in the wrong place at the wrong time and bam! I got it. It was really Momma's fault."

"In what way was it your mother's fault?"

"She should have just loved my father and put up with him. . . . She was always trying to spice up her life . . . live the life of a Bohemian, you know."

"In what way was she responsible for your father's lack of control?"

"His lack of control? She incited him to violence."

"Really?"

"Yes . . . but of course he looked for reasons to get mad. She provided them. I hate them both. God forgive me."

"Can you tell me another story? Look at the picture."

"Please, Dr. Brody, I'm not telling you stories, I'm suffering my childhood all over again . . . you know that . . . so what else do you want from me? Damn it! You sit there like a Buddha or something, all-knowing, all-kind, but you don't give a damn if I spill my guts out. Is it right for me to hate a woman who's been raped and murdered? Am I some kind of monster? Where does it all end? When I'm dead?"

"You're not a monster. You're a sensitive and fine woman. In some way you're as guilty about your mother's murder as you were about the argument between your parents. You were not responsible for their argument and you're not responsible for your mother's murder. There was no way you could have prevented it. You could not have protected her. Thoughts of murder are not the same as committing a murder. All children wish their parents dead at some time or other."

"Yes . . . once Momma opened the door to my bedroom while I was playing with my dolly . . . I was warming her under the covers, between my legs . . . I didn't know what I was doing . . . I had often felt that same sensation while rocking back and forth in my bed when I couldn't sleep. Momma came in and put her hand on my forehead. It was warm and sweaty. Then she pulled off my covers and took the doll away. 'Naughty, naughty,' she said, 'you shouldn't be playing when it's your bedtime.' I felt utterly ashamed. I was sure she had discovered my secret and would tell Daddy. I never did it again."

"Never?"

"Until recently. I read a book that helped me."

"And all those years you were punitive toward yourself?"

"I was busy being a good girl."

"What is being good?"

"Good is being the way people you love want you to be."

"Do you really believe that?"

"Not really."

Allison Kent felt shame when she was discovered masturbating by her mother. Seeking solace by fingering one's personal "security blanket" is not a crime: it is a dip in the salty sea . . . a sniff of eternity . . . a return to piscine beginnings . . . a toss among moonlit sheets at high tide. Putting a doll between one's legs is not perverse. Whether or not one's playmate is real or an effigy, there can be no objection in using this innocent fetish to allay infantile sexual needs.

A brisk walk, a good bowel movement, a short dance to radio music also contribute to a sense of well-being, and may be just as important to a masturbatory novice.

However, *not* doing something does not mean that one represses it. To *do,* or *not to do,* is always a matter of choice. Unfortunately, at times, the choice is forced on us by the frightening or aggressive maneuvers of another person. If we have made a choice in fear, it becomes, to be sure, a fearful choice, but a choice nevertheless. Fear has a greater influence on human beings than sex, dreams, hunger, or thirst. Fear has to be dealt with first! If one cannot deal with it, one gives in to it and becomes a person who cannot live life to the hilt; perhaps a nonorgasmic person, or one who finally relates only to a fetish or some form of punishment. To become healthy, Allison would have to reject her parents' values. I think she can.

# 12

---

Only Allison's heels had been injured (when they had scraped along the driveway to the emergency room) but they were healing: rough crescents of dead skin that had protected the abrasions were ready to fall off.

"It's too cold to wear open-backed shoes any more," she said. "I can fit into my boots again; am I happy!"

"Good. Good. What've you been up to these days?"

"Improving my acting." She said this mysteriously, while picking at her heel.

"Found a new school?"

"Same one. Didn't want Rueshames to think he'd scared me away."

"Brave girl!"

"I almost didn't . . . but I wanted to get back at the bastard."

"I don't blame you."

"I prepared an improvisation. Got the idea from a book Rueshames had in his room. . . . This lady in a garter belt, black silk stockings, and high heels is squeezing some terrified guy with her legs."

"You improvised around that theme?"

"Uh-uh . . . I tricked Rueshames into being my partner. . . . He was very prissy about it."

"Tricked him?"

"Oh, yes . . . I threatened to report him to the head of the department if he didn't cooperate . . ."

"I suspect that wasn't necessary."

"Then he asked me to try something more advanced."

"What was that?"

"A head scissors. The class loved it. His face got all red and I kept squeezing because he didn't ask me to stop . . . I didn't even notice it when he lost consciousness. Well, I hadn't ever done it before. . . . Three of his cervical vertebrae were crushed, and his spinal cord is involved. He may never walk again."

I was incredulous. "Allison, say it isn't so!"

"Cross my heart. The man's in New York Hospital for tests. He's not allowed to move . . . or can't move; one or the other. When I visited him he thanked me! That's how crazy he is. He said he'd never forget what I'd done for him. And then his wife walked in."

"My God!"

"I thought, Now I'm going to get shot, but as you can see, I'm still here. . . . The woman's a literary agent; she wants me to write a book about what happened to Momma. What do you think of that! It's going to be an 'as told to.' She says she can get me an advance in the six figures before a line is written!"

"That's all she said to you?"

"Oh, we had coffee and she explained that she didn't care what her husband did, as long as he didn't do it with her; that they had a marriage so open you could sail the *Queen Mary* through it; that the only thing she worried about was the day one of their daughters would find his private hoard of salacious material."

120

"What about your acting?" I asked. It was all so ridic-
ulous; she was neither an actress nor a writer, yet that was
what she was being encouraged to do.

"My acting?"

"There are other schools."

"I won't have time."

"But you've never written a book."

She threw me a dirty look. "Don't you think I can do
it?"

"Well, yes, you can."

"Do you think I can do it because it's something anyone can do?"

"No . . . I think you can do it because you really want
to . . . money is a mighty motivator."

"Dr. Brody, if my mother could keep a daily diary,
part of which you have read, certainly I can dictate an
account of our relationship and the way I lost Momma. It's
in my genes."

"You're right. I wasn't allowing for the genes."

"It won't be a snap, I admit. Paula's loaning me a tape
recorder, and someone will be transcribing the tapes. She
knows a writer who'll help me organize the material
. . . that's the way it's done, you know."

"Are you convinced that you really want to do this?
It's a painful procedure."

"I want to get Momma a beautiful stone for her grave
with the money . . . gray marble with an archangel watching over her."


This world in its present shape is not the only possible
world (said Mr. Paul Klee). His conviction that a work of
art is experienced as a "process of formation" is an insight
I had applied to my experience as a psychiatrist. Through
the process of formation, which may be a process of layering, one may change oneself and the world. I am not
speaking merely of surface effect; when things change

121

shape there is usually some monstrous or unwelcome ac-
cretion pushing up from within: a tumor, a mutant fetus,
a roast swallowed whole to satisfy the empty python
greed for love. This is changing for the worst, this is the
kind of layering that mocks life.

Layering also keeps things warm and hides progress.
The last layer is always thought to be the true layer; it is
the seen layer. That is why a separator of layers is a
searcher for truth (the sum of one's layers is the summing
up of a life). Change occurs whether or not one wants
change: the internal time clock ticks according to a prear-
ranged schedule. As in spy movies, people either meet as
arranged or are prevented from doing so by being blown
sky-high.

Everything happens in time. First the tick . . . then
the tock. This is the metronome that keeps pace for those
of us who fall easily out of step. Between the tick and the
tock falls the layer, yes; this is the way we experience the
world so as not to shiver. And every time I, Mathilda
Brody, peel away a sticky layer, the wind whips in, and a
patient trembles. The world in its present shape might be
the only possible world, since it re-creates itself in its own
image. I owe these reflections to Allison Kent.

"You mean you haven't read the papers?" Harry
shouted into the phone.

"No, I haven't."

"I'm screwed, Mathilda . . . the Lanyard paintings we
bought are fakes. . . . The man's disappeared."

"Take a deep breath, Harry, and say 'Ommmm,' then
talk to me."

"Don't kid a kidder, Mathilda; breathing deeply
won't help me . . . I'm probably going to be fired."

"But why? You didn't do this on your own. Tom
Brockton was in on it too, wasn't he?"

"Tom's in the hospital with a heart attack. When Lanyard left, he took Tom's lady love with him. It's a fucking complicated mess!"

"Stop fuming for a moment and think logically. If Tom's in the hospital, they need you at the museum . . . you won't be fired."

"Not immediately, but in the near future."

"Frankly, Harry, how could you have made such a mistake?"

"Easy."

"I don't know what to say. I'm sorry for you, dear."

"Thank you, Mathilda."

"And remember, 'This too shall pass.'"

"Not until they find the bastard and get the money back."

"But they will, they will. The world's a small place."

"Not when you have traveling money, Mathilda. They may never find him."

"Never say never, Harry."

"The man has connections all over the world."

"You're much too agitated, darling. . . . Why don't you come over this evening? I can't talk to you now."

"Never mind, Mathilda, I've got to learn to handle my own problems . . . I can't keep running to you."

"That's very mature of you, but I don't believe you mean it."

"I do . . ."

"How are you going to handle your own problems, Harry? Something fishy's going on, and I don't mean poached salmon."

"I'm busy tonight . . ."

"Another woman?"

"A call girl. I've never had one."

"Welcome to the world of man . . . I hope you have a good time."

123

"I hope so too . . . but I have a splitting headache."

"It'll go away, darling. Let me know how things turn out. I love you."

"I love you too, Mathilda."

# 13

At first Jesús had not slept in pajamas, he'd kept his jockey shorts on, and every morning he'd try to wash them out in the small washbasin in his bathroom. Twice the sink had overflowed and water had dripped down to the floor below.

"Why don't you just put them into the laundry bag and let the maid do them later?" I asked, annoyed at him for ruining the rug in his room . . . the water had seeped in there too.

"I could do 'em," was all he said.

It may have been that he was self-conscious about his stained underwear: the pale lemon color of semen could be removed only with bleach. I wondered what he thought of when he had his orgasms: Brunetti (their youthful ritual masturbations)? Agatha Kent? Young girls glimpsed in girlie magazines? Or me?

"Be more careful, then," I answered; "my neighbors don't appreciate being dripped on . . . and I don't want my rugs to rot . . . which is exactly what will happen if that rug in your room keeps getting wet."

"Take it out," he said, "if you care more about a rug than me."

"What on earth are you talking about! I don't care more about the rug than about you . . . but that's no reason to let it be ruined."

"You should trust me not to do it again. The water was an accident, Dr. Brody. I forgot it was on."

"How did you forget? Weren't you right there? Watching the lake become a waterfall?"

"I was lookin' at the TV you lend me, and I got interested. It was a scary show, but it was real good, and it give me ideas."

In a bath one may be, if one wishes, King Tut afloat in a moat, or *The Grapes of Wrath* in a bath . . . but the water must be body temperature. Yes, body temperature is a necessity. The water that the body (in part) is composed of and the water in the bath must be 98.6° Fahrenheit. This is not an arbitrary decision on my part; for the ego to dissolve, the submerged person must become one with the tepid ocean of time: suspended blissfully within a womb-tomb. This is curative. Putting the ego to rest is the same as collapsing a diseased lung so that the entire organism may heal itself and live.

Every evening before bedtime, Jesús took a bath. After the bath, wrapped in a large, soft bathtowel, he'd allow Raissa into the bathroom to sit at his feet. Sometimes I'd be allowed in too, to dry his hair. Then one evening Jesús chased Raissa out.

"Why?" I asked.

"Maybe she got the devil in her."

"What do you mean?"

"I seen this movie on TV where this puppy was really a hound from hell. You look in his eyes and you die."

"You think that Raissa is a devil?"

"Could be. First that dog on TV was a cute little pup

126

that lick your face and do sweet things, but then when he grow up, all hell break loose. The maid get locked up in a smoky room, the neighbor's dog get torn apart, and the neighbor hisself goes swimmin' face down dead! Even the girl and boy get spooked by the dog they love. So who knows? Every seven hundred years the devil pick a dog to live in. Maybe he pick Raissa this time."

"Raissa is just a dog. . . . You think she gave you the evil eye?"

"Well, I want to give her the benefit of the doubt, Dr. Brody, but when she come into the bathroom with me I feel funny."

"How do you mean funny?"

"Like I gonna do somethin' I shouldn't."

"Like what?"

"Say, there you go again, pretendin' you don't know what in my mind."

"I don't. I'm not able to read thoughts. I'm not a magician."

"Seem like you are. Another thing I see on a TV program explain what magic is. Magic is getting people to look in the wrong place at the right time . . . so maybe when you read my mind, I don't know it."

"No way, Jesús. Your thoughts are your own and if you don't tell me what you're thinking, I have no way of knowing."

"You mean you don't know I like to jump your bones?"

"You have sexual feelings toward me? That's entirely natural, Jesús."

"It ain't fair. I know you my doctor, and you don't mean to be a cocktease, but that the result of it. You make me hot."

"Neither I nor Raissa can make you do anything. It's your idea. The dog is a dog. And I'm a doctor."

"You're a woman, Doc."

"Yes, I am," I agreed.

"Well, thanks, but if anything do happen sometimes, maybe you should get rid of Raissa. She gettin' bad."

What Jesús had seen in Raissa's eyes were the cataracts of old age. The ignorant and the superstitious, out of fear, have a tendency to ascribe infirmity to the work of the devil: e.g., epilepsy as possession by evil spirits. They are right.

Bloody footprints all over the house. Not only on the floor and rugs, but on the couch, pillows, beds . . . Raissa! One of her paws was bleeding. When I examined her paws I couldn't find the cut. There was no glass on the floor. I hadn't broken anything . . . it was a mystery.

"Did you break anything?" I asked Jesús. He hadn't.

Well, I decided, there must be something stuck deep in one of her paws. Jesús, very upset, told me to take her to the vet's right away. He couldn't bear to see her suffer.

"She's not suffering," I said, "or she'd be making a fuss . . . you'd know it if something was hurting her."

Dr. Kohlmar said it was a tumor. He removed it and put a bandage galosha over her foot. He also said not to worry if Raissa pulled it off. "It may be malignant," he said. "On the other hand it may not reappear. I've stopped the bleeding."

Jesús took her right into his room and comforted her. "You're okay. You ain't gonna die. Nice old doggy, I'll take care of you."

"I've invited your mother to bring some of that food you've been craving," I said.

He looked up, surprised. "I don't know if I'm ready for that, Dr. Brody. What you want from me?"

"You deserve visiting privileges," I said.

"She cries when she see me . . . I told you that . . . call it off, Doc."

"She'll be here in a few hours. Why don't you make yourself pretty. Bought you a new shirt." I threw the shirt on the bed.

"Did she say what she's cookin'?"

"No."

The fragrance of food (lots of garlic) rose through the elevator shaft and entered the apartment before Mrs. Allendez had put a foot in it. When I answered the door, she was there, holding a big brown paper bag with a grease stain at the bottom.

"Some of the gravy's slopped over," she apologized, "but there's still enough left." She glanced into the living room for a glimpse of her son. "Jesús, he knows I'm here?" she asked.

"He'll be out soon, he's fixing himself up for you."

"He don't have to do that," she sighed. "I'm only happy to be able to see him. I miss my boy, Dr. Brody; sometimes I can't hardly get through the day without thinking about him."

Mrs. Allendez had prepared a fine meal: soupy rice, black beans, steak cut very thin with garlic pounded into it, sweet fried plantains, sliced avocado salad with slender loops of onion festooning crisp quadrants of iceberg lettuce, and for dessert there was an egg-rich flan topped with an amber lake of caramelized sugar. "It's more Cuban-style than Puerto Rican," Mrs. Allendez explained, "but it's Jesús's favorite meal." She looked tenderly at him. He avoided her gaze, burying his fork in a crusty slice of plantains.

"Thanks, Ma," he said softly.

I could see tears fill her eyes. . . . She still could not understand how her gentle son had committed such a crime. The admonition "Why did you do it?" lay in Mrs.

129

Allendez's mouth like so much roughage being chewed into absorbable pieces with the steak. There were other questions, improperly masticated, fallen between cheek and gum, unable to be swallowed: "What if someone had done it to me?" "It is as if it *were* done to me," she answered herself, and then, "But I love my son." She blushed with shame remembering Mrs. Kent on the stoop, in the supermarket.

"How're things at home?" Jesús asked.

"Not so good," she answered, "couldn't be worse."

I offered her a cold bottle of beer. "There's wine if you prefer," I said. She took the beer, a Mexican brand with two XXs identifying it.

"Not bad," she said.

"There's more; I bought a six-pack."

"Whatdya mean, not so good?" Jesús asked nervously.

"Al and me, we're splitting up. I couldn't take it no more."

Jesús looked up from his food. "That piece of shit!" he said angrily. "Why'd you wait so long? Why'd you let him do them things to me!"

Mrs. Allendez lost whatever contact she had established with him: the nice meal, the tender looks. "You don't understand," was all she said.

There was a dark spot under her right eye, a fresh bruise. Makeup had not been able to hide it. This souvenir would be reabsorbed; not so the rage that had placed it there. It had given her the courage to kick him out.

Jesús shoved the plate of food away and buried his face in his arms.

*"No debo desaparecerme,"* his mother said softly.

(I must not allow myself to disappear.)

*"Tengo miedo,"* Jesús whined into his wet sleeve.

(I am afraid.)

Mrs. Allendez put her arms around him to comfort him. *"Qué pasá? No importa."*

130

(What is going on? It does not matter.)

He turned on her. "I hate you! I hate you! I'll always hate you! I hate everybody!" He pulled away from her, almost knocking her down; rushed out of the room.

"Jesús!" she called after him.

"He'll be okay," I said.

"He hates me," she cried. "I done everything wrong. . . . What good is my life now?"

"He doesn't hate you," I said. "He feels he doesn't deserve your love."

"No," she replied sadly, "he hates me."

"Next time it'll be better; I hope you'll come to see him again. He had to get it out of his system," I explained.

"You think so?"

"I'm sure of it."

Before she left I introduced her to Raissa and told her how much Jesús cared for the dog; how he fed her and was teaching her a trick. It cheered her. "He always had a soft spot for animals," she said.

"He reads a lot too, and listens to music. He wants to learn guitar," I said.

"Guitar?" Her eyes widened. "His real father was a musician. . . . Jesús must take after him."

How eager she was to contrive a semblance of hope, to create it from whatever information I held forth. That he might someday become a musician (though he did not even own a guitar) liberated her momentarily from melancholy. There was nothing more I could do for her.

On entering the gloomy room where Jesús stood (like a Pietà, one tear glued miraculously to his cheek), he asked if his mother had left.

"Yes," I replied.

"Did she leave the flan?"

"Of course she did."

"That's good," he said, "I'll eat it now."

131

# ALLENDEZ, JESÚS, FILE

## SUBJECT: REUNION

Regarding the reunion between the patient Jesús Allendez and his mother, I claim partial success; there had been anger and guilt as there must be when there is a "return to the scene of the crime." The *scene* should be understood as "the way things had been in the past," the *crime,* as the separation of Jesús from his mother (interpreted by him as her wish to see him dead . . . as proof that he was "bad").

The offering of flan (a gift from the blissful past when he had been the "good" son, and the focus of love) was an offering to Jesús of the possibility that he might live simultaneously in the past and the present . . . and become whole.

It is important to note that Jesús longed for closeness not only with the good mother (preabandonment), but with the natural father "disparu." His threat that he might run away was actually the unconscious hope that he would one day be fused: return to the country (cunt-tree)/fatherland (penis) where he had once basked beneath a lactating penis-breast. Regression was necessary in order to remove his fear and resultant resistance.

I became aware of my own changing role (within the therapeutic context), of being forced to assume characteristics of the "absent mother." And of having to withstand attacks (verbal, attitudinal, and physical) for my maternal aspects; to be the object of hurt and angry feelings; to be expected (at the same time that he was trying to destroy me, "the bad mother," postabandonment) to continue to care for him until such time as he would be able to live simultaneously in the past and the present . . . to believe in himself and to mend the fragmentation that had occurred.

The business of the phantasmic father might never be resolved; phantoms come and go at will; they fend for themselves, and when they summon the haunted subject (in this case, the grieving son, Jesús) he is impelled to follow, often with tragic consequences.

The mother abandoned by the father abandons the child, after which the child abandons himself; a never-ending pattern of nonforgiveness (a threatening chain letter) that I must help Jesús to break.


"They've found Lanyard," a relieved Harry said. "He was hiding out in the basement of his Palm Beach estate."

"Good . . . now things can take their proper course."

"Annie McFadern was with him too."

"Annie McFadern? I don't recall . . ."

"The woman he took with him . . . Tom's amour."

"Oh, yes. How is Tom?"

"Still in intensive care. Don't think he's going to make it."

"Who is?"

"Are you unhappy, Mathilda? You sound so pessimistic."

"Just a momentary lapse of energy. . . . So, they found Lanyard in the basement of his home?"

"His basement is not an ordinary family recreation room, Mathilda . . . nor is it an austere locked fortress."

"No?"

"No! It is equipped for his 'special' needs to give and receive pain. Annie McFadern had to be released from a four-poster bed that she was tied to, when the police managed to gain entrance. Sordid! Imagine, the man loved the delicate watercolors of Demuth, the fine line of a Rodin nude, the rich bloom of a Nolde flower painting at the same time that he was loving the bleak pleasures of a torture chamber."

"Speaking of erotica, Harry, how did you make out with that call girl?"

"She was beautiful, knowledgeable, compliant, clean,

and sweet. . . . She turned me off. Healthy creatures frighten me . . . I paid her and sent her home."

"You know, Harry, you're about to become a candidate for the loony bin. Why don't you talk to someone . . . I can recommend . . ."

"Honey, there's nothing I can't handle on my own. Is it my fault that only *love* blows the trumpet for me? I want to be in bed with you."

"No, you don't; you want to control me."

"I'm having a tough time doing it long distance."

"What are you doing tonight?"

"Going to hear some jazz at the Eatery. Why? Want to come?"

"Just asking . . . have a good time, and don't drink too much."

"Your concern touches me."

"I knew it would."

# 14

"Do you remember any more Grandma stories?" I asked Jesús.

"Yeah. Grandma, she tell me the story about there was this scorpion who want to get across the water, but he can't swim, so he ask Mr. Frog to take him. 'Please, Mr. Froggy, take me across the water, 'cause my family over there and my kids in trouble.' Mr. Frog didn't want to. He think the scorpion would sting him, but then he got to thinking about it, that the scorpion wouldn't sting him because then they would both drown. So he say, 'Okay, Mr. Scorpion, I take you across to see your family. Climb on my back.' The scorpion jump right on Mr. Frog's back. He was very happy because when he get across the water he would be able to help his kids who was in trouble. But in the middle of the water the scorpion do sting Mr. Frog. Mr. Frog was very surprised, 'Hey, why you do that, Mr. Scorpion? Now we both dead in a second.' 'I know,' the scorpion say, as he was drownin', 'but I couldn' help it.' You see, Dr. Brody, it were his nature. He had to be hisself, even in the face of danger. So, lots of things what I do I can't help it neither."

135

"You can't come into my room until I tell you," Jesús said. He had something up his sleeve . . . had been working on a surprise for me all week. I hadn't a clue as to what it was.

"Don't take all night," I said impatiently.

He had put a sign up on his door: ENTER AT YOUR OWN PERIL! (a warning more appropriate for a roomful of third rails, or rabid bats). We had become "close." I liked having him in the house. Our regularly scheduled sessions had given way to just living together and taking care of what came up when it came up. His enuresis had not returned, he was no longer hallucinating, his friend Brunetti was a topic of the past. His anger, though, was still a source of worry for me . . . his tendency to act out . . . and lately the discovery of his dirty underwear in my clothes hamper.

When I asked him about the displaced laundry (there was no necessity for him to use my hamper, he had his own laundry bag hanging from a hook inside his closet door; it was not full), he claimed to be helping me. "Keep it all together for the maid." I understood it as a bid for intimacy; if skin to skin is impossible, the next best thing is underwear to underwear: semen-stained jockey shorts thrown helter-skelter into an odorous domain of worn female lingerie achieves the desired intimacy.

There were instances of physical contact that I had, at the time, explained away as having been accidental: the way he had leaned over me as I read the paper, his mouth sending warm gusts of air down my neck; his habit of brushing against me in the hall, staying just a second too long before continuing on his way. He had become solicitous of me at night too, knocking at my bedroom door, then entering swiftly to ask if I'd like a drink of water, or a snack, since he was going to fix one for himself. Once he had come in before I had had a chance to ask him to wait, and found me standing naked, about to dress for bed. A

136

later remark of his, "You don't look like a doctor," brought this pitiful invasion of my privacy back to me. How young he was! How full of notions; he wanted to prove to himself that I was a woman like all the others: he had to demystify me. This did not make me happy, since I could not tell when he would be done with demystifying.

"You can come in now," Jesús said, smiling. He was obviously pleased with himself. A sheet was hung across one side of the room, and behind the sheet was a lamp. Jesús led me to a seat in front of the sheet. "Your seat, madam. I sincerely hope you enjoy the show I have prepared for you this evening."

The lights were turned off, leaving us in darkness. Jesus went behind the sheet, put on the lamp, and made an opening speech.

"This evening I have prepared for you what I think will be wonderful and great in the best tradition of shadow puppets. For yes, dear audience, with the help of my puppet friends Tootsie . . . Take a bow, Tootsie . . . and Dawn . . . Take a bow, Dawn . . . we gonna put on a supersensational show. Don't think that shadows ain't real. They are. They can sing and dance and do whatever actors can do. And so forth. The so forth is X-rated, so if you are the kind of person who is easily offended, please take this opportunity to leave the theater now. Thank you."

Jesús used his hands as the shadow puppets.

### SHADOW PLAY WITH SHADOW FIGURES
by
Jesús Allendez

*Characters*

TOOTSIE . . . A male about sixteen years old.

137

DAWN . . . A female about eighteen years old.

TOOTSIE *is walking down a street in Washington Heights near the Golden Moon Coffee Shop.*

TOOTSIE: It sure cold out here in the street. I rather be fuckin' some hot chick who don' mind me jumpin' her bones.

*Along comes* DAWN. *She has a sexy walk.*

DAWN: Hey, what you in my way for, stupid?

TOOTSIE: That no way to talk to your admirer! I wanna see your tits and be sweet to you and all.

DAWN: So okay. But why we don't have some fries and coffee first and I see if we hit it off. You look real cute, but maybe you a jerk.

*They enter coffee shop.*

TOOTSIE: Hey, look, I'm the best lover you ever see. Give me a chance. You got it easy. You can pick and choose, but the ladies they don't go with me when I want.

DAWN: I can't help it if you comin' on to me about my tits and what else. I gotta be careful. Why I should be wastin' my time with a kid who ain't got nothin' to offer me 'cept his prick? I askin' you!

TOOTSIE: Don't good character matter? I somebody very special. I dig the flicks and I dance good. And I got brown eyes. I learn how to cook too, and I sure appreciate your dimples, and I overlook your pimples.

DAWN: Naw . . .

TOOTSIE: Naw? You come in here and I pay for your food and you ain't gonna give me nothin'? Who do you think you are?

138

You think your shit don' stink, right? You think you just ain't in the human race.

DAWN: You got it. I'm too foxy for you. I the model type drive you nuts in my bikini. I lookin' for the suave type who ride me aroun' in his limousine, wear gold chains, own a duplex apartment with terrace and who carry credit cards that ain't stolen. A guy who treat me like dirt but give me Arpège.

TOOTSIE: So a guy like me ain't got a chance with a girl like you?

DAWN: You hear me loud and clear.

TOOTSIE: So a guy like me ain't got no chance in this life?

DAWN: No.

TOOTSIE: So a guy like me he oughtta kill hisself.

DAWN: That up to you, sucker fucker. But sure as night follow day, and day follow night, if you don' get it together somebody goin' put you away, if you don' put yourself away. How you know I am just a nice piece of friendly ass? How you know I not gonna mass-murder my way through life? You don' know what I got in my bag, baby. It a neater heater and a man beater.

*She takes gun out of purse and aims it at* TOOTSIE.

DAWN: Treat me nice and you turn to ice!

*She shoots the gun.*

DAWN: Hey, man, why you duckin' under the table? Ain't no bullets in this fucker. Made it in arts and crafts class outta a potato.

TOOTSIE *rises from behind the table. He grabs the gun out of* DAWN's *hand. He shoots* DAWN.

139

DAWN: *(groans)* I dyin', for Christ's sake. Fuck you . . . hey, whut your name?

TOOTSIE: I just the avenger who passin' through. Go where the wind blow. When it stop, I settle down. The world got twists and turns of fate, and it twist and turn guys like me. It were just your bad luck to meet me when I feelin' real bad . . . and look what happen.

DAWN: I'm thirsty . . . I could use a Coke.

TOOTSIE: When I say so long, I don't run errands . . . so goodbye and stay dry, bitch. . . . It coulda been a good thing. Yeah, really. But it wasn't meant to be. *(He speaks to audience)* And so, dear audience . . . you who have stay with me through thick and thin . . . I ask you: Why do fools fall in love? And why do the rest of us don't?

"How you like it, Mathilda?" Jesús was proud of himself.

He had used my first name the way one inserts an intimate detail into traffic directions. It jarred. After weeks of stammering his way through Dr. Brody this, and Dr. Brody that, he had achieved parity with the use of my first name.

"I think it's good," I said. "Lots of energy, humor, and truth."

"It good enough to be in a real theater?"

"Sure, but you've got to write more . . . longer stuff."

"Then I go right to the top?"

"There's no guarantee of that."

"If there's no guarantee, then why should I bust my balls?" Jesús asked.

"Work is its own reward," I replied. "Try it, then see what happens."

Raissa had begun coughing, and lay listlessly around the house. She ignored balls rolling across the floor that

140

had formerly tempted her; she came dutifully to her bowl of food, but did not empty it; even her tail-wagging did not have much lift to it . . . and so I surmised that she was truly ill.

Dr. Kohlmar took tests and diagnosed heart worms.

"When did she get them?" I asked.

He said it could have been any time, or probably in the summertime when mosquitoes are around.

"Mosquitoes?"

"The disease is spread by mosquitoes."

"Why didn't you notice that Raissa had heart worms before?"

The answer that a dog may carry them for years before the disease is evident did not satisfy me. Yes, we couldn't save her and she died soon after. I knew that Jesús would have a major reaction to her death . . . that it would bring back the memory of his own dog Doggy. Raissa died in the hospital, so Jesús was not able to comfort her (and himself). He would not believe that she had died.

"I brought her collar back," I said; "you can keep it."

"Don't want no damn collar. Want my dog. Why'd you bring her to the hospital where you don't know what they do to her? Maybe they keep her for experiments! Shit!"

I showed him the certificate of death, a crisp duplicate of the original naming Raissa as the deceased (also giving information such as date of death, cause of death, age of animal at death, to whom she had belonged, and the state and zip code where she had died). Another veterinarian, not Dr. Kohlmar, had signed the paper.

"I don't care what it says," Jesús exploded.

I put my arms around him. "I'm so sorry. I miss her too. I had her for a long time."

He snuggled his head into the crook of my neck,

wetting it with tears. "She didn't even have time to learn any tricks. It would have been cute," Jesús said.

"She gave you her paw once, remember?"

"No, she didn't, I picked it up."

"I saw her. You asked for her paw and she gave it to you."

"Yeah?" His face brightened. "I didn't realize it."

"And you played tug-of-war with her . . ."

"I know . . . but we coulda played more."

He let me hold him. It was pleasant.

Project funds have dried up . . . the Projects Committee, after examining my casebook, came to the conclusion that the results achieved, and the concomitant amount of money spent to achieve those results, were disproportionate. Was a dry bed a significant achievement? The disappearance of a nasty hallucination important? The emergence of a creative talent from what had once been a meticulous, nonspontaneous, obsessive-compulsive, valid? And how, without seeming insane myself, could I compare the expensive video equipment I had acquired during the Allendez investigation to something as scientifically understandable as a microscope or a tongue-depressor?

I knew that there were rumors circulating about me: that I was sexually perverse, a thief, and a liar whose scholastic degrees were bogus. The sexual perversity charge originated many years ago after I had married a former patient (and divorced him soon after). There was no forgiveness for me. The bogus degrees had been a youthful prank: to me the Ph.D. stood for *P*eople *h*ave *D*reams . . . my explanation was not believed.

The big question was, How to tell Jesús that the state wanted him back? How to prepare him? As for myself, it was a misfortune I could hardly bear. He was not blood, but he had become my only family.

142

# ALLENDEZ, JESÚS, FILE

Having rejected his mother, lost Raissa, not regained Brunetti (memories of his friend were fading; only the anxiety remained), experienced a transference that manifested itself as sexual desire for me (the I rejected), Jesús was ready to remove his rage from escrow. How he would do this I'd conjectured before. I hoped that the picture card he was about to look at and analyze would aid me in discovering plans he had not yet made.

1. *Description:* A naked man is clinging to a rope. He is in the act of climbing up or down.

2. *Manifest Stimulus Demand:* a. An adequate accounting includes the man and the rope plus an explanation of the setting. This normally implies a reference to whether the man is going up or down the rope.
b. Other details frequently noted include specific reference to the muscles or to nudity. Not infrequently the background of gray will be referred to in identifying the scene.

3. *Form Demand:* The impression of movement is strong here and, while in essence the only major form consists of the man, the rope, and the background, it would seem that attention to the movement is an essential part of the stimulus.

4. *Latent Stimulus Demand:* This is an extremely useful picture because it reflects the subject's concept of the relation of the individual to his environment and images of his prowess or vulnerability to environmental forces. Narcissistic, exhibitionistic, and competitive ideas are readily aroused here, as are notions of fear and escape.

5. *Frequent Plots:* The man may be seen as an athlete showing his prowess or as an escaped prisoner. Normally, the figure is the hero, and the sympathy of the storyteller is with him.

That is, the escaped prisoner is normally escaping from evil forces. Most frequently he will be seen as going up the rope.

6. *Significant Variations:* It is useful to note the nature of the environment in which the figure is found as well as whether or not other figures are introduced to assist, hamper, or observe him. The subject's desire for recognition and display, or his fears of vulnerability should be noted. Attention may be paid to the possible descriptions of nudity or physical build.

"The guy in this picture is definitely weird!" Jesús commented. "What he doin' mountain climbing without his clothes? It sure to be cold up there, and if it ain't, there gonna be some wild animals ready to bite his skinny ass minute he show hisself up there."

"Then you think he's climbing up?"

"Way to go man! . . . but that gray sky do worry me. It gonna become a blizzard and blind the poor sucker, but he got to keep goin'. He can't go back no more. They waitin' for him down there. Maybe they cut his rope so he fall."

"Why are they after him?"

" 'Cause he's a bad dude! He so bad his own face scare him in the mirror . . . but he ain't in shape. He got no muscles."

"Then how does he manage to stay on the rope?"

"He develop some technique in stir. He don' wanna be a prisoner. He wanna be free."

"What about the wild animals on top of the mountain?"

"Don't worry, there's a sensational lion-taming chick up there who see the dude coming and want to save him. She gonna slay the lion and pull the dude to safety."

144

"It's safe at the top of the mountain?"

"Sure. They gonna go to her candy house. Smoke weed. Talk away the time of day . . . party. Like that."

"Then what?"

"Do there have to be more? Man, that's heaven."

"Can he keep running away? What about his enemies?"

"They can wait. One day he be back to square things."

"Was the danger worth it?"

"Once you get a taste of it, it don't leave you. So you gonna be in danger when you have to, and if you die, that it."

"Lion-taming chick" = Dr. Mathilda Brody

"Bad dude" = Jesús Allendez

"Wild animals on top of mountain" = repressed and "dangerous" impulses within Jesús Allendez.

"They waitin' for him *down there*" = down there is death and eternity: the unknown; the endless fall broken only by the bodies of those who gave up before reaching safety.

The climbing rope is life. The poor, naked sucker is Jesús Allendez, inching upward in total anxiety. Someone may cut the rope . . . wild animals may attack him from above . . . he may tire ("he ain't in shape") and allow himself to fall out of life . . . but he wants to live . . . he wants to be free. Prison = death. Freedom = heaven. Jesús Allendez would do anything to be free . . . he is willing to die trying to live. As he said at the end of our last session, "Once you get a taste of it [freedom], it don't leave you. So you gonna be in danger when you have to, and if you die, that it."

He does not know that the "lion-taming chick" has been ordered to return the key to his cage to the authorities. Outside of a miracle (rescue by helicopter, for instance), the prognosis is bad for Jesús. If only, like the spider, we humans could spin additional threads of life, one stronger than the next, attachments bonded firmly to the broken ends!

# 15

---

Jesús was away at the facility for two days to get a medical checkup (to satisfy their records, and to make sure he hadn't contracted VD, TB, the big C, or shot H). Harry insisted that I get out for a good time.

"Tonight, I'm taking you to a show," he said.

"What show?"

"To the hit show that made sexual fantasies respectable."

"You sound like a promo."

"I'm reading from the flyer . . . want to go?"

"Why would anyone want to make sexual fantasies respectable? What can they mean?"

"No dirty words, no nudity. It's a "bring your mother" presentation . . . I'm curious."

"I won't be ready till after eight."

"We can come late."

Harry does not cross the street when the light says "Go," he likes to zigzag his way through traffic urging me to follow him. This is dangerous stuff; more than once I have escaped injury by inches. This is the way we went across the street to get to the show, so I was reasonably upset with him.

"You want to get me killed," I said.

"You won't get killed if you're careful," he answered.

The enactments Harry and I had missed were about punishment: a schoolteacher forces her stupid pupil to stay after school. She entices him by raising her stockinged leg, and allows him to sneak a look up her skirt. When she catches him looking, she orders him to pull down his pants, puts him across her knees, and spanks him. In another sketch, a young wife becomes a "bad" girl: drops things, bothers her husband by asking him to stay home for sex instead of going to a party. He allows himself to be taunted until he retaliates by putting her in manacles which he calls toys, whips her with a narrow birch rod that he then draws between her legs and smells, after which her ankles are also manacled and attached to chains which are a staple of their bedroom, and she is hung upside down. All of which she enjoys immensely. These miniplays were described to me over a glass of wine during the intermission (when we came in) by an eager young man who thought it all so fine he was going to purchase some of the toys he had seen on stage, for his own affairs. "The wrists don't rub too raw," he explained with some delicacy, "if you put Vaseline on first."

Harry and I found space on an occupied, plump, red cushion just as the final sketch began: Imagine a bachelor pad. Imagine a young bachelor nervously waiting for his date. Now, imagine that his date is a tall, slender, blond manikin . . . the same kind one sees being dressed and undressed in store windows, sometimes minus a head, sometimes minus a limb or two. The date arrives. It is the department-store dummy, obviously prettily dressed by someone with a theatrical conscience. The man greets her warmly. They dance. He throws her onto some upholstered blocks that serve as a bed. He unbuttons her blouse and exposes her breasts. As he undresses her, he accuses her of being a slut, a whore, a bitch . . . of being so hot that she always wants it . . . of being so insatiable when she gets it, that she can't get enough! The dummy, set in her ways, takes no notice of him. Finally satisfied that his date is all the things he says she is, the man rapes the dummy. After he rapes her, he tosses her on the floor as if she were a used Kleenex. He zips up. Slicks back his hair. Scene over.

The actor who portrayed the male character spoke afterward to the audience. He claimed that the show carried an important message to those who were ashamed of their fantasies . . . that it was okay to fantasize if no one got hurt. I did not speak up, since my opinion would have been far too clinical for the occasion, but in fantasy, there is always someone who gets hurt since the one whose needs are greater will have to coerce the indifferent partner to satisfy the fantasy. The show we had just seen had been advertised as "Another Way to Love." It was an enactment of total alienation: another way to hate. I did not understand this perversion of the word love. Well, I did understand. Love was the word that drew the audience into the theater. The woman who had acted the part of the dummy explained that the show was about the most intense *sexual communication*—developing your deepest sensuality and *sharing it* with *someone you love!*

"Guilt has always been big business," I said to Harry, "and I suppose it's more popular than ever now, judging from that young audience."

"They come to see flesh redden and quiver," Harry said, "but it's strictly hetero . . . a retrograde retread of hetero sex . . . hardly worth $7.50 . . . and the *vino rosso* was atrocious."

Perhaps it is not all right to fantasize.

I have already given too many of my patients permission to fantasize.

Is fantasy the word or the picture?

When we dream do we see the dream, or are we the dream?

Why do thoughts take place in the head?

If thoughts are intangible, why do we have them?

What is the thought process? It is not a computer.

Why do I want to reinterpret and change things?

Am I able to change myself? Because my mother died of the cold, do I yearn for warm weather?

Isn't all inner life improvised? Yes, around a theme.

"What were you thinking just now?" Harry asked before we went to bed.

"I was thinking this and that, nothing important."

"You had an intense look on your face."

"Oh . . . I was wondering whether there was any juice for the morning."

That night I was able to gather material for my essay on premature ejaculation, when Harry, who was not usually a chronic orgasmic speedster, came without warning.

Advanced thinking believes there is no such thing as premature ejaculation, that this is sour grapes on the part of a partner whose sexual time clock is slow (not the Seiko quartz variety, a paragon of accuracy) and who finds it inconvenient to be correcting the "time" while the premature ejaculator is already having his cigarette and a cup of coffee. This is a healthy state of affairs. Do my medical colleagues, the urologists and sexual therapists, advise a masturbator to practise *masturbatitis interruptus?* Or advise him to consecrate the fiery organ with (over-the-counter) anesthetic ointments to distract him from pleasure? No. So where are we? Is the ideal and highly touted simultaneous orgasm a desirable, or even a possible, goal for consenting, copulating (male versus female) adults?

In line with advanced thinking, I too believe that there is no such thing as premature ejaculation: what is good for the onanist is good for the twosome. How together must togetherness be? Once we understand that sexual intercourse is not what gives the female pleasure anyway, the pressure will be off.

My position is still not a popular one, though there has been lip service in that direction, and it will earn me no credit in higher analytical circles. . . . I am already in a kind of professional limbo since my superiors no longer recommend cases to me, and I must find my own (such as the Allendez case, and the Kent case). However, when I lecture at universities, where experimentation and originality count, I am regarded with the respect due me.

"Dr. Brody, why you always so busy lately? We ain't sit down and talked for three days now," Jesús complained.

It was true, I'd been avoiding him, unable to bring myself to tell him the bad news. Isn't the bearer of bad tidings often struck down as if *she* were the bad tidings herself? I had bought Jesús a gift: a silver ring set with a semiprecious blue stone . . . a "graduation" ring.

"I've been talking with the people at the prison," I answered. "I tried to get them to be more lenient . . . to give us more time. . . ."

Jesús leaped up. "What you tryin' to tell me, Mathilda?"

"They want you back next week," I replied in a rush. I put my arms around him and shoved the ring into his hand. "I want you to have this."

He threw the ring across the room. "What I need a ring for? Don't go with prison clothes, do it? Tell you what, maybe I will keep it, 'cause they ain't gonna get me back!"

I had picked the ring up. Jesús grabbed it out of my

151

hands and his elbow accidentally hit me in the eye. This made him absolutely wild.

"How that feel, Mathilda? You hurtin', Mathilda? Maybe I should cut my arm off for hittin' you? Right, Mathilda? Maybe I should go drop dead . . . maybe we both die this time. Don't make no difference. Don't mean shit! Don't mean fuckin' shit!"

I had expected trouble, and here it was. Jesús rushed to his room taking with him a brass statue of Narcissus gazing into a smooth brass pool, which I kept in the living room. He threw it repeatedly against the walls of his room, tearing large holes in the plaster; he broke records, tore the pages out of books, ripped his sheets, and refused to ever eat again.

"What'd you tell them? That I raped you? That I was too dangerous to keep?" he screamed.

"No, no!" I interrupted, wanting to hold him, but keeping my distance. The eye was swelling up and I hadn't had a chance to put ice on it. "I wouldn't say anything bad about you. It's a matter of money. The city wants to end our special program."

"Money? Don't they listen to you?"

"No, they don't. I'm not the boss . . . but if the program is reinstituted . . ."

"What's that mean, Mathilda?"

"It means the decision isn't that final . . . they may yet find the money for us to go ahead. I wouldn't give you up if I didn't have to."

"That's what you say! That what they all say! 'I had to leave you, Jesús. I don't have the money, Jesús. It for the best, Jesús. Goodbye, Jesús.' You think I'm a dumb bastard? You think I don't know I'm too bad to be desirable? You want me so much, how come you don't fight for me?"

"I will . . . I have . . . I won't stop. You've come so far."

"Yeah, sure."

"You're able to say what you mean, you have strong

152

feelings, you're a talented artist, and those TV skits you made up are marvelous . . . I have high hopes for you."

"I don't, not if I go behind bars. I'd forget who I am in stir. In stir everybody watch the same TV program, and you want to change it you start a argument. I love my TV. That's where I got my start in life, and look like that's where I'm gonna finish up."

"You don't actually know that, darling."

"Hey, you called me darling. Why in hell you so sweet? Make it hard to leave. Why don't we run away somewhere, where they can't find us?"

"They'd find us."

"I read in one of your magazines about Argentina . . . criminals go there, and nobody can find 'em."

"Forget it."

"You got another guy you want to move in with you? A better case?"

"Where'd you get that idea?"

"Nowhere."

"It's not true. When you leave, I intend to limit my caseload and devote more time to writing."

"About me?"

"You, and others . . . I won't use your real name, though. . . . Maybe your story will help other young people to understand themselves."

"Don't give a damn about other young people, they gonna get in trouble anyway. What make you think they gonna read your book?"

"Some might . . . but what's more important is that the people who judge these kids might be influenced to see them as people like themselves, and not as felons."

"Well, as long as you gonna change my name, Doc, you should tell the truth about my life, don't make it too much like a movie . . . that decision come up, I plan to do the script myself."

"Swell . . . come on, help me clean your room now."

"First I'll tell you about the dream I had last night . . . okay?"

"Okay."

"In the dream I was a little baby without no clothes on. You kept putting me in and taking me out of a drawer. When I cried, you slapped me. So I stopped crying. Then I was on the steps of a house, waving to a kid I knew, but I didn't know who he was and he was smiling at me. I tried to warn him not to come no closer, but he kept coming. The earth opened up and swallowed him. I could see him going down, but there wasn't nothing I could do to save him. I remember thinking, how come he's coming to see me in my house, when he lives in such a nice place?"

This was a prescient dream of disaster. I did not play too happy a role in it either. Jesús had been sensitive enough to realize in advance of my announcement that something was wrong. I remained calm so as to continue the session with some degree of professionalism.

"What did this visitor look like?"

"I don't remember, but I was happy to see him. When the earthquake come it make me sick. I felt as if I was dying from the dirt in my mouth . . . but it wasn't me."

"I see."

"He was bringing me a present, I think, in a paper bag. It was something I wanted very much."

"If you had three wishes, what would they be?"

"Hey, only three? Let's see . . ."

"Three is all you get, so make them important wishes."

"First, I'd want Raissa back here with me . . . then, I like to party with my friend Brunetti . . . and the big three is, not to be a prisoner! There's my three wishes. You gonna make 'em come true?"

He looked at me defiantly, then began gathering the things he had thrown around. I brought in a three-ply

154

trash bag, large enough to hold three gallons of trash.

"You got room for me in there?" Jesús asked.

That evening I lay in bed thinking about my former passion for the African violet . . . my loving care of them until they hardly seemed to need me; they had been so healthy, so beautiful, so profuse . . . an affront to other kinds of existence. How relieved I had been not to care for them . . . to substitute the artificial . . . and how sly of me to have hidden a single red rose made of silk in a bouquet of real roses. Only I knew the character of this self-inflicted pain: many years ago I had presented my mother with such a rose (costing only 25 cents, bought from a street vendor) for her birthday. She had been happy with it, but I had been embarrassed because it was so cheap a gift. I couldn't allow myself to forget it. Lying in bed I told myself that all this had a bearing on my relationship with Jesús . . . that I was actually glad to be getting rid of him . . . I had gone as far as I could with him too. It occurred to me that when he was gone, we would write to each other, and that his letters would be like my one bloody rose: a reminder of how narrow and ungenerous I really am.

And then Jesús knocked on my door.

"I'm frightened, Mathilda," he whimpered.

"Come in, then," I responded, immediately guilty.

"I can't sleep. Can I sleep with you?"

"You can stay here awhile."

"What if I fall asleep?"

"I don't know . . . well, maybe . . . the bed's big enough, I suppose."

"I always wanted to sleep with someone who like me," he said softly.

He got in and lay on his back.

"Comfortable?" I asked.

"Sure, and I getting to feel a lot better. Your room is pretty, just like you, Mathilda. . . . Hey . . ."

"Yes?"

"How was your mother to you? You ever see your mother?"

"No, not any more. My mother died when I was a teenager, like you."

"Oh . . . she dead . . . oh, too bad. Was she very old?"

"Not so old. She was sick though, and poor."

"Your mother was poor? Then how you get to be so rich, Mathilda?"

"It's not something I like to talk about."

"You can tell me . . . I told you lots of things. Just between us . . . let it all hang out, Mathilda."

I hated that stupid phrase which prompted me to imagine an unzipped, unbuttoned squadron of human beings flying above the earth, their sexual appurtenances swaying in time to the official Air Force song.

"Come on, Doc. Trust me."

"It happens to be a difficult subject for me, Jesús."

"So take your time; talk about something else. Did you have a good day today? Was your breakfast fattening?"

"So, now you're the analyst?"

"I learn fast."

"Yes."

"So, Mathilda, you say your mother was poor? How did that make you feel? As if it your fault?"

"I didn't live with my mother, I lived with my father. Mother lived alone . . . she wanted to be independent. She wouldn't accept any money from my father. That's how much she feared him."

"Understandable. Understandable."

"We didn't know it, but her landlord wanted her to pay more rent. He harassed her."

"Hold it, Mathilda . . . would you care to explain that word harassment. It ain't familiar to me."

156

"The word means to bother someone. The landlord stopped giving heat. It was winter . . ."

"Sonofabitch!"

"The pipes froze and burst . . . Mother froze to death . . ."

"Just like you read in the papers about old people."

"When they found her she was packed in ice."

"She stay fresh a long time that way," Jesús said, breaking the unhappy mood.

"Why'd you say that? It was very mean," I said.

"You gettin' too sad, Mathilda . . . it scare me; I don't like to see you with your feelings."

"But you asked me to tell you about my mother, Jesús . . . I'm human too."

"Maybe, but not to me, Doc. You somethin' else. You the strong one."

"I'm just pretending. I was taught to pretend. Analysts die of cancer, heart attacks . . . they go mad! I give what I can but I'm not the Rock of Gibraltar."

"What rock is that? Central Park rock? Or what? Like the magic rock that don't break in half? Somewhere I heard about a rock with a sword in it. . . . So maybe that mean some rocks can break open and still be strong."

"Once a rock's been split open it's wide open and can be demolished."

"Okay, you got me again, Mathilda . . . what's demolished?"

"Destroyed altogether."

"Come on, Mathilda, shape up. You don't have to be that strong! I apologize for being so tough about your mother and all. Here's a kiss for your trouble."

I held him in my arms. It was a lovely thing to do. How nice it would be to have a child of my own, I thought.

"Tell me a story," Jesús asked, his Mickey Mouse face close to mine.

"If I do, will you get back into your own bed?"

"I promise," he whispered, "unless you want me to cheer you up."

"I'm cheerful enough," I replied, ignoring the sexual innuendo.

He rolled to his back, closed his eyes, and waited for the story.

To a certain extent my attitude toward tragedy is that it is far more comic than any comedy . . . and that is how I was thinking about Jesús and myself in my bedroom, on a queen-size mattress, waiting for a story. How deceptive certain scenes are.

"Tell me a story about beer," Jesús asked. "Try it, and if I get thirsty you gotta get me a beer."

"I'm game . . . well, let's see. . . . Once upon a time a go-go dancer went to a bar in East St. Paul on her day off, where she met another woman and they both had some beer on tap. Then they went to another bar where they ordered large bottles of Sappora, a Japanese beer. Later the two stopped at her apartment before going to another bar. The second woman found two babies, a three-month-old girl and a sixteen-month-old boy crying in their cribs. She also found seven dogs and several cats. The place smelled of animals and defecation and there was defecation in the children's hair, on their bodies, and in their cribs. There was nothing but sour milk on hand, and the mother told the second woman to fix bottles for the children with the milk anyway. The mother then offered to sell the children for a glass of beer apiece.

"The second woman took the go-go dancer across the street and bought her two beers. She took the children, brought them to her mother, and her mother cared for them ever since."

Jesús had fallen asleep. I watched him for a while wondering at what point in the story he had dozed off . . . and then I fell asleep myself.

About 3:00 A.M. I woke up all wet. Jesús had peed in

158

bed, something he had not done in months. I did not wake him, but stayed there in the sopping linens, marveling at how Jesús had suckered me into his scenario. In the morning he said that it had been me who had wet the bed. When I tried to deny it he became angry with me and left the room.

I received a disturbing letter from Dr. Kohlmar concerning Raissa; he had, he said, found freshly healed wounds on her corpse that had been made with a sharp, narrow instrument, possibly a razor or a knife . . . cuts that had been easily overlooked since they had been obscured by hair. He was concerned, he said, because of his role in not having discovered them soon enough, and did I have any ideas on how this could have happened . . . some canine-phobic patient left for a short time with the dog? . . . some street person attracted to Raissa as she strained against her leash outside a supermarket? . . . an overworked servant seeking revenge on her employer? He left it to me and sincerely hoped that I would investigate the matter, since cruelty to animals was something he had fought against all his life. He begged me to join his crusade, especially since I had been the owner of the abused animal myself. "Think how you'd feel, if it had been one of your children," he closed (revealing that I was a complete stranger to him, even after years of dealing with me as a pet devotee).

My intuition told me that it had not been I who had taken a razor to Raissa (and then wiped it out of my consciousness); nor had it been any of the other choices Dr. Kohlman had suggested. . . . Only one other person had had access to Raissa's adorable presence . . . Jesús.

Since the dog was already dead, and Jesús on the way out of my life, I did not question him about the evidence of sadism Raissa's assiduously nicked flesh bore witness to. A single, curt interrogation would help no one, not even

Dr. Kohlmar. It needed years of analysis, this kind of thing . . . the best action to take, therefore, would be to hold off acquiring another dog while Jesús was still with me. I had been thinking of bringing a puppy into the house for the week or so we still had left together.

Freud asserts that children transfer their relationships with their parents to animals; in this case Raissa carried the totemistic features of both father and mother (being not only an animal, but a bitch), and so received the acting out of both matricidal and patricidal tendencies (of which Jesús was the carrier). The concealed death sentences authored by Jesús stirred a great sense of guilt and fear in him, so much so that he had begun to doubt his own existence. Unfortunately, his sadistic behavior toward Raissa was a futile attempt to rid himself of these authority figures and to exorcise his doubt.

I even began doubting his stories about Doggy; they had been so sentimental, so obvious. . . . Was Jesús a con man? Even his dreams had not been dreamlike; it was as if he had gone through my files, read some cases, and then put a dream together the same way he had "written" his play.

Would it be easier for me to let Jesús go if I vilified him?

# 16

Allison broke her appointment with me. "Why are you resisting?" I asked her.

"I'm not resisting, I just couldn't make it."

"Just couldn't?"

"I was working on my book and the time flew . . . before I knew it, it was too late."

"Do you want to reschedule?"

"Can't we have our session on the phone?"

"I'm not at your disposal, Allison. I have other appointments."

"But this is my time. You couldn't have anything else to do now."

"I have time this evening after ten. If you want to see me, come then."

"All right, Dr. Brody . . . that's what I'll do."

"I've got a great writer helping me," Allison said. "His name is Mr. Singer."

*"The* Mr. Singer?" I wondered why the master storyteller would be working on an as-told-to with Allison Kent.

161

"*He* thinks so," she answered.

"Are you talking about the Pulitzer Prize-winner who eats in dairy cafeterias?"

"He eats in cafeterias, I know that for sure . . . but the Pulitzer? He's written handbooks on how to assemble stereo units for Eiko Electronics. You should read the man's prose: so lean, not a word wasted. Is there a Pulitzer given for exceptional work on pamphlets?"

"Have you seen Rueshames lately?"

"I did the right thing and sent flowers, but I don't have the stomach to visit him again. When I was there he made me an indecent proposal. . . . He asked me to kill him."

"Kill him?"

"To smother him by sitting on his face. . . . Luckily a nurse walked in, or I would have been guilty of a mercy killing."

"Okay, Allison, so why don't you come out from behind the smokescreen and talk to me . . . you're only wasting your own time."

"I am talking!"

"Oh?"

"I really am. If I'm not talking, who is?"

"A few days ago we were discussing some things about your attempt to play the piano . . . your difficulty with scales . . . particularly with the left hand."

"That's not important; just a problem with my circulation: whenever I touch the keys my fingers get tingly. Sometimes they grow numb."

"Numb?"

"Um-hum, numb . . . stopped me from playing real good. . . . Mostly the left hand bothers me . . . I relate better to the upper register . . . to the treble clef . . . to its shape."

"Its shape?"

162

"Its pregnant shape; that fat belly resting on the staff. . . . Do you know that the notes of the treble clef, the ones that lie in the four spaces, spell the word 'face'?"

"What about it?" It was obvious to me that Allison didn't want to *face* the music, and that music was *pregnant* with meaning for her.

"I don't know . . . why does it bother me? On the other hand . . ." She giggled and held out her left hand. "On the other hand, the other hand is my left hand."

"Yes, it is." The left hand is sinister or ill-omened. . . . It plays music that is written for the bass clef . . . the clef that clefts asunder . . . Allison's left hand did not want to "tickle" the ivories . . . the female genital is cleft . . . "Tickling" the ivories is a substitute for either masturbation (a problem area for Allison) or foreplay (or four play . . . face has four letters). Allison experiences numbness in her left hand, thus, inhibition occurs below (the bass clef).

"What notes lie in the spaces of the bass clef?" I asked, hoping to find additional clues that would help us tackle this difficult hodgepodge. I hadn't used free association as a therapeutic technique in a dog's age. In fact, free association was in current disrepute, since whatever was spontaneous had to be rerouted through the analyst's limited handbook of interpretations before being accepted as valid.

"Let's see . . . A . . . C . . . E . . . G. That's it. A crazy sentence used to go through my head," Allison said.

"Crazy?"

"Should I say it?" She twisted in her chair, not wanting to say it.

"How can a sentence be crazy?"

"It is, it is! Doesn't make sense, but it's here in my head."

"I'm sure it will make sense eventually, Allison . . . say it."

"All right. . . . A cunt exits gore. Isn't that a crazy

163

sentence? That's what I read into the bass spaces . . . the lines are even worse. The notes are G . . . B . . . D . . . F . . . A."

"How much worse can G . . . B . . . D . . . F . . . A be than A . . . C . . . E . . .G?"

"God break Dada's friggin' ass. I'm so embarrassed, I could die."

"Nothing to be ashamed of, not yet anyway, my dear . . . so let's try to liberate these words from the elusive past."

"There's more, Dr. Brody."

"I'm game."

"I forgot to name the lines of the treble clef."

"A significant lapse, no doubt."

"E . . . G . . . B . . . D . . . F . . . Every good *boy* deserves favor . . . that's the way they help you remember the notes in school. Why isn't it Every good *baby* deserves favor? Makes me so mad! Boys get everything, even the treble clef! They get her pregnant. She gives birth to a son. She loves him more than her daughter. He dies. And the daughter is loved less instead of more."

"You come from a very musical family," was all I could bring myself to say. Until I could get a magisterial grasp on what the hell was going on with Allison Kent and the Western scale, my response would have to be minimal. But then I found myself commenting, "God break Dada's friggin' ass! You surprise me, Allison; you have a flair for integrating religion and obscenity within one small sentence."

In the foyer she turned to me, bright-eyed, happy; not at all bothered by her strange revelations after all. "I want to tell you a joke," she said. "It made me laugh all the way down here."

"I'd love to hear it, I need a good laugh."

"It's a short joke."

"Shoot."

164

"My mother knew I was going to be a feminist the second I was born. When the doctor hit me, I hit him back!"

"Thank you for sharing it with me," I said, opening the door.

"You didn't like it?"

"I tried to," I said.


Allison had been struggling with an impulse to have sexual relations with Mr. Singer. "He's very attractive," she'd said, "and he's still in love with love."

"That's a definite plus," I'd responded.

"He brings me flowers, and we both love tuna sushi. What do you think of May/December romances, Dr. Brody?"

"What do you think?"

"People think I'm his daughter."

"Does it bother you?"

"It infantilizes me."

"How do you want to act?"

"Like an adult . . . Mr. Singer is not a father substitute. I swear."

"No."

"I get very depressed after I see him."

"You get depressed?"

"We have a good time, go to a movie, and then I'm depressed."

"Yes?"

"It's as if, because I'm having a good time, I don't care about Mother. It was like that when I had to pack up her clothes . . . I mean her 'going out' clothes. As long as they were there in the closet she was alive, you know. Her death wasn't real to me. Every day I had to convince myself that she really was dead. When the closet was finally empty, I believed it . . . not even the condolence cards had convinced me. She's really gone, isn't she?"

165

"Yes . . . and you deserve a life of your own. Punishing yourself won't bring her back."

In the dream Allison had brought to the last session she had been wandering around in a large empty room, perhaps the recreation room of a mental hospital, carrying a large bolster. She'd noticed a patient who was dressed poorly, and had on a pair of old, worn shoes. She'd stood near him and inadvertently touched his "fly" with the bolster she was carrying. She'd then put the bolster down on a bench. She and the patient had sat down on another bench. She'd felt that he expected her to undress and make love to him. At this point, to fool him, she had looked into his eyes, as sincerely as she could, and said, "I don't have to take my clothes off. My soul is naked."

I was in my study thinking about popular trends and what they reveal about the adolescent . . . how the huge radios carried by some, blasting out music to call attention to themselves, had been replaced by the Walkman: a set of tiny earphones attached to a lightweight, portable radio that could be hooked onto a waistband or belt, almost obscured from view, pouring music directly into the ears of the wearer . . . still, a status symbol (especially if worn with a pair of gaudy shoe-skates, or added to a jogging outfit), and the phrase blatant nonblatancy had just begun to form in my mind, when Jesús entered and stood over me, trying to see what I was writing.

"I thought I told you to knock before you come in . . . I'm working!" I said, irritated.

"I need some money, Mathilda! I want you to give me some money."

"You can't demand money just like that! I'm not a bank. I can't give it to you. You have no right to . . ."

"I got a right to do whatever I please. This here gives me the right, Doc!" He pulled a knife from his pocket and

166

crouched, holding the blade ready for an upward thrust. I froze. This is not happening to me, I thought, Jesús would not attack me. He was just testing me. It was a desperate, yet ineffectual move on his part. I stood up. The knife nicked my hand swiftly. "I hate you, Doc," Jesús screamed, "you're a disappointing bitch, same as all the others. You don't give a damn if I drop dead. You ain't ever took me out for even a walk, or to a restaurant, or a movie like you go to with that Harry jerk. You coulda sneaked me out. Who woulda known? We coulda dated like real people. It was up to you. I gave you your chance when we was in bed, but you treated me like a baby. I ain't no baby, Mathilda."

He twisted my arm and pushed me against the wall. His strength amazed me. I looked around automatically for Raissa, then realized she was dead and gone, and I was alone with Jesús.

"I know you're not a baby, Jesús."

"Yeah." He grinned; his eyes cold. It was hypnotic, this view of Jesús, a Jesús I did not know (a Jesús we had talked about in our sessions as if he were dead or had taken up residence in some far-off, inaccessible place, and would never come back . . . yet here he was). "I'm big where it counts!" he screamed. "This here. This here's what makes me a man." He grabbed my hand and held it against his fly. He had an erection. "You think you know about rape? You don't know nothin'. Playing around with me, huh! Shit! Bet you think you know all about me because I talk, talk, talk, talk, talk to you . . . talk, talk, talk . . . just talk! I don't care what I say to you. I say anything to you. You just a bitch! You gonna get your big chance to be a whore."

"If I'm a whore, you certainly don't have to threaten me with that knife. Whores want it all the time, don't they?" I tried to be in his head, to think the way he did,

167

all the while beginning to move away from the wall, cautiously.

"Don't move your ass, Doc . . . wanna call the cops? Won't do you any good. I already killed one lady, said she was gonna report me. See this knife? It your kitchen knife that I see you slice meat nice and thin with; I know how to use it too . . . it never leave my right hand. I slice you till you're dead, Mathilda. I hate you, Mathilda. I hate you, baby!"

He shoved me to the floor and ripped my blouse. His hand pulled at my panties. He still had his erection. I could feel it as he pressed down on me. I did not fight back. I still did not believe that this was a rape . . . a clumsy, unfortunate lover perhaps . . . but not a rape. He wanted to terrorize me, but when I remained calm, he lost his erection. "Drop the knife, Jesús. You don't really want to hurt me, or yourself."

The blade circled the flesh around my eyes, and finally I became frightened. Jesús regained his erection. "You see too much, little lady," he said softly, romantically, "you do see too much . . . but I been looking at you too; all them days in your unbuttoned blouse, make me hot. I'm gonna fuck you good and then you be dead! But first you be blind!"

I didn't care what was happening down there (afterward I hurt; I suppose he was big; I'm rather small), I became one big brain, still trying to think for him, be him. "Your mother was really bad to you. She hurt you, didn't she?" I said. "She was always picking on you."

Tears moistened his cheeks. "She treat me like garbage, the whore. Do you think I'm garbage, Mathilda?"

"No, no! You're a good person. Let me help you, Jesús; put the knife down . . . oh, please."

He lifted himself off me, in a daze. "Give me one reason for living, Mathilda, just one." The knife was still in his hand: his knuckles white as boiled potatoes, hard as bone. I rolled away from him and stood up.

168

"Do it for me. You're all the family I have," I pleaded. "Everything changes. Look, I know you're depressed; please give yourself a chance. I promise not to tell anyone what happened. . . . You could have killed me; you didn't. This time something inside stopped you."

"Mathilda, I can't stand the idea of being in jail for twenty-five years before I even come up for parole."

"I know, but that's the way things are, and you'll have to stand it. I'll visit you, you'll learn new things in jail, when you come out, you'll still be young, with lots of years to go."

His grip on the knife loosened; it fell to the carpet.

"You won't tell?"

"I promise."

"I'm thirsty, could I have a drink of water?"

I brought him the water, and with it a tranquilizer. He swallowed the pill without objection. "You don't think I'm garbage?" he asked again.

"Of course not . . . now come on, I'll help you to bed; you must rest now . . . sleep it off."

The evening was spent with me on guard against what had already happened: as I went over things I could have done to stop the rape, a disturbing train of thought took hold of me: Had I wanted it to happen? And if so, why?

I am a competitive person, who has never been afraid to explore areas that others (in my profession) have avoided. There is no documented instance of any psychiatrist laying her body on the line in the interests of science (I am not speaking here of Madame Curie, of course). In the true spirit of a pioneer, I managed to recreate conditions identical to the ones that sent Jesús to me in the first place: an authentic situation in which I was able to observe the psyche of the rapist and the victim as an insider . . . thus, I was in possession of privileged information with which to swell the Allendez dossier. This intimate and terrifying investigation should (after I sorted it out) be

169

invaluable to those who come after me . . . however, to be honest, I must add here that I had been an abused child, psychically unable to react effectively against violence: one of my mother's favorite games was hunter and rabbit, in which she was the hunter and I the rabbit. She was an excellent hunter, adept at finding me wherever I was hidden, and entirely convincing in her role as a champion bagger of game: when she caught me, she'd beat me mercilessly for destroying her garden. Mother was certifiably insane . . . but not always. Going through analysis twice, I have not been able to heal myself entirely, but have managed to live a life entirely dependent on myself (we have but one life to live, and we might as well live it). In a life of service to others, it is Mother I am trying to cure.

I could have won Mother's love if I had let her kill me.

I could have destroyed Jesús Allendez twice over if I had let him kill me. I was angry enough to kill *him* as he slept, but it would have destroyed me. He is garbage. His stench proclaims that he is ancient, fermenting matter . . . a truckload of waste on its way to the dumping ground . . . human debris that must be buried at last.

There, I got that off my chest. Allison would be proud of me, a friend of the victim at last.

The following day Jesús kept to his room. I looked in on him a few times, saw that he was busy or resting, and returned to transcribing my notes. It was as if nothing unusual had happened between us. Before dinner, I decided to begin a discussion of what had happened and why. Jesús was not in his room, but I found a disturbing note on his desk.

*Dear Dr. Brody,*
    *I don't want to go back to jail so I'm leaving . . . and I also can't face you after yesterday. It threw me, to see I done something like that to you. I thought I was okay, but you see, I'm not. Not your fault, not no one's. I took some*

*money from you that you wouldn't give me. I need it.*
*Someday I pay you back. Thanks for being my good friend.*
*I know you are, no matter what I said when I was loco. And*
*please don't tell the police yet, or try to find me. I'm doing*
*what I gotta do.*

*Sincerely,*

*Jesús*

I did not notify the police even though he had flown the coop. I even applied for an extension of time for Jesús to stay with me (as a cover-up). The days dragged on without either a call or a note. I was worried. This was not like kissing my African violets goodbye.

"Have you heard anything?" Harry's voice echoed my concern.

"No . . . nothing."

"Any idea where he might have gone?"

"He did mention Argentina."

"How much money did he take?"

"Not much, dear . . . not much at all. That's what worries me."

Allison rented a room at the Hotel Dover on the Upper West Side, "where Mr. Singer and I can work in peace; I'm going crazy trying to remember the details of my childhood, Dr. Brody. Mr. Singer says to make it up because it's not the important part of the book; Mother's murder is. That's what'll make it sell. . . . Oh, and I think I'm falling in love with Mr. Singer . . . he's so funny! He bought gold glitter and pasted it over the liver spots on his hands, and he wants to go out to discos with me."

"He sounds lively enough. How're things otherwise?"

"The hotel is full of creeps . . . I thought maybe I'd meet some interesting people in the lobby, or in the elevator, but no . . ."

"No?"

"Except yesterday, I saw some guy at the magazine kiosk . . . it's a convenient place for me to buy my candy and newspapers . . . it's right in the hotel . . . but this guy, when he turned around, I could swear he was Jesús Allendez."

"You're at the Dover Hotel?"

"I was, yesterday. We decided to take some time off. Mr. Singer's invited me to spend the weekend at his son's place in Great Neck."

"Enjoy yourself," I said.

I knew it would do no good to ask the hotel registration clerk whether a Mr. Jesús Allendez was registered there; Jesús would have changed his name. Harry said he'd be free that evening and if I wanted to, we could hang around the Dover Hotel lobby together on the chance that Jesús would show up.

We spent three hours on an itchy upholstered couch in the lobby, alert to each and every person who entered or left the hotel; no Jesús.

"I've had it," Harry sighed.

"I'm game for tomorrow night, how about you?" I asked. I had a hunch that if we kept at it, our vigil would produce Jesús.

We were not able to resume our search. Others took over in the wake of tragedy.

### IN THE MIDST OF PANIC

*One Deadly Twist Blamed in Tragic Hotel Blaze*

New York (AP)—Fire investigators today blamed one fatal twist for the welfare hotel fire that took the lives of 40 people.

Yesterday's ravaging blaze broke out in one of

the rooms and sent thick, mushrooming smoke throughout the 12-story building.

Investigators analyzing the nature of the fire at the Dover Hotel said its damage might have been limited to the floor on which the fire was discovered, but that fire doors had been propped open by the workmen brought in to do repairs. Most of the dead who were trapped in their rooms died of smoke inhalation.

Yesterday officials said that a preliminary investigation revealed that the fire had started in a mattress accidentally ignited with a cigarette. The bodies of some of the victims have been tentatively identified. Until the list of victims has been completed and next of kin notified, names are being withheld.

An odd fact concerning Jesús came to light when I spoke to the fire captain who had directed the investigation of the blaze. It seems that Jesús had been saved, but then inexplicably had run back in, and died. He'd been found huddled in a corner of his room with his arms around a guitar!

Mrs. Allendez repossessed his few scorched belongings, among which was the suit he was to be buried in. She said she had made arrangements to return to Puerto Rico with him, and that she would remain there.

As soon as Allison found out, she called. "I suppose you already know that Jesús Allendez died in the fire . . . I was right, I did see him that day at the kiosk buying toothpaste and razor blades. . . ."

I'd expected her to announce dramatically, "Revenge is mine!" or even, "The score is evened now," but what she said was, "And you devoted so much of yourself to him . . . I'm sorry, Dr. Brody, I really am."

I went to the Allendez, Jesús, File to reminisce; pulled out an unexamined item that had been stored for future reference.

## STAMPS SATURATED WITH LSD

The Police Department urged parents yesterday to caution their children that small stamplike paper tabs saturated with LSD are being distributed in and around grammar schools.

Lieut. William Hurt of the department's public-information division said that the tabs, about a half-inch square and made of blotting-type paper, are decorated with colored pictures of Mickey Mouse depicted as the "Sorcerer's Apprentice" . . . The objects are "fairly well saturated" with the hallucinogen, he said, and if they are licked or chewed a child could suffer a severe case of hallucination.

My Mickey Mouse (Jesús) had been my apprentice and learned nothing. He had taken the broom (not magical in itself) and attempted to sweep the room clean (a room pulsing with oceanic torment); wave after wave engulfed him as he tried to hex this destructive torrent with half-remembered spells.

"You know something you won't tell me," he'd shouted, swallowing water. In the midst of this chaos I'd tried to say the right words and return things to their proper places: the puppy he had loved as a child and lost romped miraculously across the room and into his lap; a grandmother's kiss had tumbled from the ceiling where it had been pasted by the advancing tide and placed itself (fulgent) upon Jesús's cheek; his father, a resistant spider-web that had persistently reestablished itself from corner to corner as Jesús chased it with the broom had stopped to fasten itself within a corner of the room's ceiling, becoming (as we spoke) a safety net (and no longer the perilous tissue through which Jesús had fallen); his friend Brunetti had returned, jerking off (companionably) into the sands of time (that filthy, waste-strewn beach).

Whether or not I had been a sorcerer producing

these hallucinations (a commonplace stunt for sorcerers) for Jesús, I do not know, but the severity of the patient's symptoms had called for extraordinary measures: the return, one way or another to him, of those things that had innocently dawdled in the scum-gray waters of the libido, before going down the drain. The air-filled wings made of plastic Baggies, Kojak's tootsie-pop, Superman's sibilant *Sssssss* emblazoned on a shirt . . . even Dracula's ardent fangs . . . and a true-to-life enactment of a pickup in Washington Heights, belonged to Jesus; he had a right to them just as he had a right to crippling guilt, or the disability of no guilt at all.

These borderline cases are so unpredictable; they can haunt one for a lifetime.

# Addendum

---

PSYCHOANALYSTS GATHER FOR TRIBUTE TO
MATHILDA BRODY
*by Rex Osa*

Many of the nation's preeminent psychoanalysts gathered
in New York yesterday to pay tribute to Mathilda Brody,
who, with Cela Gass, helped establish the field of eclectic-
inaudible juvenile psychoanalysis. Dr. Brody died November 23 of a presumed heart attack, one hour after an unknown assailant had thrown a rock at her, opening a gash
in her forehead that required forty-five stitches. She was
describing her attacker when she suddenly succumbed. At
the time of her death, she and Dr. Hank Edelweiss, a col-
league, were preparing an abstract: *Machine Fantasies—
Where Robots and Other Man-Made Monsters, Machine
Gods of Our Time, Are Examined as Expressions of a Uni-
versally Distributed Male-Pregnancy Fantasy,* to be presented at an international meeting of psychoanalysts in
London.

"Mathilda Brody's life could be taken as an exemplar
of the life of a psychoanalyst in that impossible profession,"

Dr. Edelweiss said in a brief encomium at the memorial.

Dr. Edelweiss said Dr. Brody's colleagues had not always found enduring value in her capacity to "translate psychoanalytic understanding and insights into an obscure language of her own, but that even temporary relief given by her to troubled people made them feel that they had a sympathetic and resourceful ally in their difficult lives. Her practical guides, individually charted for each individual case, gave advice that helped to remove guilt and other masochistic distortions, e.g., incompetency in the pseudo-stupid, from the lexicon of her clientele."

In a message to those at the memorial, Cela Gass said that she was present in spirit, but that poor health prevented her from journeying from London. The memorial to Dr. Brody, who lived on Central Park West in Manhattan, was at the Goornisht Memorial Chapel, Broadway at Sixty-first Street, chosen because of its capacity to hold a large crowd of mourners, its accessibility to transportation, and the recent renovation of its interior in the style of the Mark Rothko Chapel in Houston, Texas.

## Development of Clinical Work

During the vigorous intellectual years of the Nixon administration, the creative burst that gave birth to eclectic-inaudible juvenile psychoanalysis enveloped Dr. Brody and Dr. Gass. It was then that Dr. Gass—together with Dr. Brody and Dr. Edelweiss—developed the clinical and theoretical work that would shape the formal development of juvenile psychoanalysis. Dr. Brody, in New York, had started one of the world's first formal subterranean cranial sound-system laboratories and out-patient head-set programs for adolescents.

Dr. Mathilda Brody, Theodore Brody's daughter, had made the fundamental discovery that listening enabled juveniles to augment their inner life according to stereo sound patterns and musical enjoinders, that conspicuous audio input, remastered and mixed in the adolescent's

177

mind, was equivalent to free association in adult psychoanalysis. At that time she began to focus her concern on the clinical aspects of treating adolescents.

"She began to develop her own style of working with young people, which was certainly part and parcel of the establishment of adolescent 'flux' psychoanalysis," explained Dr. Edelweiss, the director of the Sound and Unsound Study Center at Columbia, which was founded by Dr. Brody's father, Theodore Brody.

## Father Was a Barber

Born in North Carolina in the late thirties, Dr. Brody grew up amid the intellectual isolationism of the formative years of psychoanalysis. Her father, not yet convinced that psychoanalysis was a fit profession for a grown man, since it would place him in a compromising position vis-à-vis beautiful young women whom he would then have to resist, remained a barber for a number of years; among his clients were Freud's children, and Reik's daughters. It was T. Reik who convinced him to give up his tonsorial duties to become a psychoanalyst.

"Dr. Mathilda Brody followed in her father's footsteps just as Anna Freud had with Sigmund. She was a very good teacher," recalled Dr. Gass. "She was a very lucid, down-to-earth person; always gracious even when she thought you were totally wrong."

## Violence on TV

Although Dr. Brody concentrated mainly on the clinical aspects of sound and unsound adolescent "flux" analysis, she contributed a central study to the field of adolescent violence, by illuminating the possibilities for predicting a young person's reaction to violence on TV, particularly on adolescents who had already committed crimes. Her expertise was eagerly sought in court cases concerning these matters, and she was rapidly achieving a national reputation at the time of her death.

Dr. Brody continued working until she died, leaving many projects unfinished, including a major study of the experience of being the one left behind: mother, father, sister, or brother of a murder victim. Her work will be carried on, colleagues say, financed by a fund set up in her memory. Those interested are requested to send contributions to: Dr. Mathilda Brody Fund, The Sound and Unsound Study Center, Columbia University, NYC.

Dr. Edelweiss concluded: "It is a great loss. She leaves a great gap. This is a death that is wholly unacceptable!"

# Editor's Note

The obituary you have just read was composed by Dr. Brody and placed in her file two years before her death. She failed in her attempt to outguess fate, since her death was not caused by an act of random violence, but by a common household accident. Dr. Brody, hurrying to answer the phone, slipped on a rug, hit her head, and suffered a concussion. Soon after, she went into coma, from which she did not regain consciousness. Also incorrect are the facts concerning her father, who remained a barber all his life, dispensing whatever advice he had to give while trimming hair. At the time of her death, Dr. Brody's colleagues still refused to acknowledge her contribution to the field of adolescent psychology, and labeled her a maverick practitioner whose unorthodox and "sensational" techniques had caused more harm than good. Her dear friend and companion, Mr. Harry Minton, claimed the body, since she had no next of kin. Students who wish to research the work of Dr. Mathilda Brody should write to the University of Wyoming in Laramie, where her papers are included in their archives.